YORK NOTES

fore

Frankenstein

Mary Shelley

Note by Alexander Fairbairn-Dixon

Longman York Press

Dedicated to my family and to a wonderful philosophy tutor, Deirdre Eadey

Alexander Fairbairn-Dixon is hereby identified as author of this work in accordance with Section 77 of the Copyright, Designs and Patents Act 1988

YORK PRESS
322 Old Brompton Road, London SW5 9JH

PEARSON EDUCATION LIMITED
Edinburgh Gate, Harlow,
Essex CM20 2JE, United Kingdom
Associated companies, branches and representatives throughout the world

First published 1999

ISBN 0–582–38231–9

Designed by Vicki Pacey
Illustrated by Neil Evans
Phototypeset by Gem Graphics, Trenance, Mawgan Porth, Cornwall
Colour reproduction and film output by Spectrum Colour
Produced by Addison Wesley Longman China Limited, Hong Kong

CONTENTS

PREFACE

York Notes are designed to give you a broader perspective on works of literature studied at GCSE and equivalent levels. We have carried out extensive research into the needs of the modern literature student prior to publishing this new edition. Our research showed that no existing series fully met students' requirements. Rather than present a single authoritative approach, we have provided alternative viewpoints, empowering students to reach their own interpretations of the text. York Notes provide a close examination of the work and include biographical and historical background, summaries, glossaries, analyses of characters, themes, structure and language, cultural connections and literary terms.

If you look at the Contents page you will see the structure for the series. However, there's no need to read from the beginning to the end as you would with a novel, play, poem or short story. Use the Notes in the way that suits you. Our aim is to help you with your understanding of the work, not to dictate how you should learn.

York Notes are written by English teachers and examiners, with an expert knowledge of the subject. They show you how to succeed in coursework and examination assignments, guiding you through the text and offering practical advice. Questions and comments will extend, test and reinforce your knowledge. Attractive colour design and illustrations improve clarity and understanding, making these Notes easy to use and handy for quick reference.

York Notes are ideal for:
- Essay writing
- Exam preparation
- Class discussion

The author of these Notes, Alexander Fairbairn-Dixon graduated from the University of East Anglia with a first class degree in English Literature. He is the English Co-Ordinator at a college in Teesside.

The text used in these Notes is the Penguin Popular Classics edition of *Frankenstein* (1818; revised 1831) published in 1994.

Health Warning: This study guide will enhance your understanding, but should not replace the reading of the original text and/or study in class.

PART ONE

INTRODUCTION

HOW TO STUDY A NOVEL

You have bought this book because you wanted to study a novel on your own. This may supplement classwork.

- You will need to read the novel several times. Start by reading it quickly for pleasure, then read it slowly and carefully. Further readings will generate new ideas and help you to memorise the details of the story.
- Make careful notes on themes, plot and characters of the novel. The plot will change some of the characters. Who changes?
- The novel may not present events chronologically. Does the novel you are reading begin at the beginning of the story or does it contain flashbacks and a muddled time sequence? Can you think why?
- How is the story told? Is it narrated by one of the characters or by an all-seeing ('omniscient') narrator?
- Does the same person tell the story all the way through? Or do we see the events through the minds and feelings of a number of different people?
- Which characters does the narrator like? Which characters do you like or dislike? Do your sympathies change during the course of the book? Why? When?
- Any piece of writing (including your notes and essays) is the result of thousands of choices. No book had to be written in just one way: the author could have chosen other words, other phrases, other characters, other events. How could the author of your novel have written the story differently? If events were recounted by a minor character how would this change the novel?

Studying on your own requires self-discipline and a carefully thought-out work plan in order to be effective. Good luck.

Mary Shelley was only nineteen years old when she completed her novel *Frankenstein*. Since then her monster has become so popular that in the late twentieth century, we see him in films, advertisements, comics and even computer games.

How is it then that the young Mary Shelley wrote a book that has become more famous than any other work of **Romantic** (see Literary Terms) literature and, indeed, herself? Her unconventional life and upbringing might give us a clue.

Parents and early years

Mary Shelley was born in 1797 near St Pancras in London, the only daughter of two prominent political thinkers of the time: Mary Wollstonecraft, the first **feminist** (see Literary Terms), and William Godwin, a radical philosopher. Ten days after Mary was born her mother died of childbed fever, leaving Godwin devastated.

Frankenstein, Walton and the monster all spend their formative years addicted to reading.

Mary grew up in a cultured environment and became an avid reader. Although Godwin was an emotionally distant father, he was a good teacher and Mary had free access to her father's extensive library. As a young child she would have also been used to celebrated writers visiting her illustrious father, including Charles Lamb, William Hazlitt and the inventor Humphry Davy. We know that aged four she and her stepsister, Claire Clairmont, hid behind the sofa out of fear when the great **Romantic** poet, Samuel Taylor Coleridge recited 'The Rime of the Ancient Mariner'.

The pursuit of knowledge is the central obsession of Victor Frankenstein and Cpt Walton.

When she was fourteen her father wrote this of her: 'Mary ... is singularly bold, somewhat imperious and active of mind. Her desire for knowledge is great, and her perseverance in everything she undertakes almost invincible.'

1812–22
Romance and
Tragedy
These are central
themes in
Frankenstein
(see Themes).
Frankenstein and
Walton clearly
share some of
Percy Shelley's
characteristics.

This period of Mary's life is characterised by adventure and death. Between 1812 and 1814 she stayed with Godwin's acquaintances, the Baxters, in Scotland. These **sublime** (see Literary Terms) surroundings aroused her and she began to write. On returning home (aged sixteen) she was to find a new visitor, the young poet Percy Shelley, who, although recently married, was to become her future husband. He was a handsome young man with flaming auburn hair, whose wild emotions, energetic imagination and intense excitement for nature, the supernatural and science (see Context & Setting) make him a fascinating poet to read. It was not long before they fell in love.

This period was a
profound influence
on the imagery
(see Literary
Terms) of
Frankenstein
(see Context &
Setting)

In July 1814 they eloped to the continent with Claire. However, both of their fathers were enraged by the illicitness of the affair and effectively disowned them. Pursued by Shelley's creditors on returning to England, they left for Switzerland in 1816 where they met the poet Lord Byron at whose villa Mary started *Frankenstein* (see Context & Setting).

Much of Mary's early life was spent trying to get to know what her mother had been like by reading her books. Mary's painful awareness of death and loss continued to haunt her life and writing. In 1815, only seventeen, she gave birth to a daughter who died twelve days later. On 19 March she had a dream; she wrote: 'Dream that my little baby came to life again – that it had only been cold and that we rubbed it by the fire and it lived – I awake and find no baby – I think about the little thing all day'.

The idea for
Frankenstein *also*
originated in a
dream.

Worse was to follow: in 1816 Mary's half-sister committed suicide, and Percy Shelley's wife drowned herself. Although this circumstance enabled Mary to marry Percy, they were never forgiven by their fathers. Mary's second child, William died at the age of three. And Percy Shelley himself drowned in 1822. By 1824, with the death of Lord Byron, Mary found herself isolated and alone.

1824–51
Writing and
motherhood

Her friends and family gone, Mary devoted her time during this period to the upbringing of her only surviving child, Percy Florence Shelley, and writing for journals and magazines. She also published the second revised version of *Frankenstein* in 1831, and wrote the futuristic novel *The Last Man*. Mary Shelley died at the age of fifty-three in 1851.

CONTEXT & SETTING

SOCIAL MONSTERS

When Shelley was writing *Frankenstein* she was reading *Emile* by a famous French philosopher, Jean-Jacques Rousseau, whose ideas inspired the French Revolution. In this book he argues that man's nature is harmless but that men are made evil by society. Men become 'monsters' by the way they are treated. However, he says that 'a man abandoned to himself in the midst of other men from birth would be the most disfigured of all'. This debate is at the heart of the book: the monster is born good but becomes wicked because people abuse and reject him. Worst of all, his creator, Victor Frankenstein, refuses to grant him his natural rights of Freedom, Equality and Fraternity.

SUBLIME NATURE

The setting,
imagery (see
Literary Terms)
and mood were
influenced by
Mary's travels in
Switzerland.

Victor Frankenstein grows up in the Swiss city of Geneva, and it was here that Mary Shelley started to write her novel. During the summer of 1816 Percy, Mary and her stepsister Claire visited Lord Byron at the Villa Diodati, from where they could see the majestic Alps. Here they also met 'Monk' Lewis, famed for his supernatural stories, and Dr Polidori, Byron's young physician. The group formed a habit of talking into the early hours, and one night Byron read aloud some ghost stories from a book called *Fantasmagoriana*. He challenged the gathering to a ghost story competition. This set the **Gothic** (see Literary Terms) tone for Mary's novel.

The storm becomes a motif (see Literary Terms) in the book.

Mary was clearly excited by the **sublime** (see Literary Terms) nature of the scenery; she wrote: 'The thunder storms that visit us are grander and more terrific than I have ever seen before. We watch them approach from the opposite side of the lake, observing the lightning play among the clouds in various parts of the heavens, and dart in jagged figures upon the piny heights.'

Climbing the Alps, she saw the *Mer de Glace* (the sea of ice) near Mont Blanc: the desolate scene where Frankenstein and his monster first meet (pp. 93–5).

MYTHS AND LEGENDS

Mary Shelley alludes to many myths in the course of *Frankenstein*.

Prometheus

There are two versions of the Prometheus myth. In the Greek version he is a rebel who steals fire from the ruler of the gods, Zeus, and a friend to humanity because he gives them 'the gift of fire' but is then eternally punished by Zeus. In the Latin version, Prometheus creates man from clay and water. Victor is a 'Modern Prometheus' because he rebels against the laws of nature by making an unnatural man because it would be of 'benefit to mankind' and he is punished for his efforts by his creation.

Faustus

Dr Faustus is an academic who rejects normal pursuits for magic because he wants to know the secrets of the universe. He sells his soul to Satan in exchange for this knowledge but does not know what to do with his

Author's life		Scientific advances
	1746	**1746** Invention of Leyden jar (prototype electrical condenser)
	1750	**1750** Jean-Jacques Rousseau expounds idea of 'noble savage'
	1752	**1752** Benjamin Franklin invents lightning conductor
	1762	**1762** J-J Rousseau's *Emile* advocates children be allowed full scope for development away from harmful influences of civilisation
	1784	**1784** Benjamin Franklin, Antoine Lavoisier and others investigate Mesmer's claims of a 'magnetic fluid' present in man
	1785	**1785** Invention of artificial insemination
	1786	**1786** Invention of 'lightning conductor umbrella'
	1790	**1790** Luigi Galvani, in experiments with frogs' legs, believes he has discovered electricity present in animal and human limbs
	1794	**1794** Erasmus Darwin's *Zoonomia* discusses spontaneous generation
1797 Mary Wollstonecraft marries William Godwin (atheist and anarchic philosopher); **Mary Godwin** born; mother dies ten days later	1797	
	1800	**1800** Alessandro Volta creates prototype electric battery
1801 Mary's father, William Godwin remarries	1801	

Author's life	Scientific advances
	1812
	1812 Invention of canned food used on voyages of exploration
1814 Mary elopes with Shelley to Continent	**1814**
1815 Mary gives birth prematurely to daughter, who dies a few days later	**1815**
1816 Mary gives birth to son William; Mary and Shelley leave for walking tour in Switzerland; meeting with Byron, who has liaison with Mary's stepsister Claire; Mary's half sister Fanny commits suicide; Shelley's wife commits suicide, Mary and Shelley marry	**1816** **1816** Invention of wooden stethoscope
1817 Mary writes *Frankenstein;* gives birth to daughter Clara	**1817**
1818 Publication of *Frankenstein;* family leave for Italy where Shelley writes *Prometheus Unbound;* daughter Clara dies in Venice	**1818** **1818** First (unsuccessful) blood transfusions at Guy's Hospital, London
1819 Son William dies; son Percy born	**1819**
1821 Mary writes *Valpurga*	**1821**
1822 Shelley drowned at sea	**1822**
1824 Mary begins work on *The Last Man*	**1824**
1830 Mary publishes *Perkin Warbeck*	**1830**
1831 Revised edition of *Frankenstein*	**1831**
1851 Mary dies	**1851**

power. Tormented by the deal he eventually perishes in hell. Similarly, Frankenstein relinquishes his family for the pursuit of secret knowledge, and, working in isolation, creates a creature that he abandons. The monster revenges himself, like a devil, by destroying Victor's family and friends.

The Fall of Man

Adam and Eve in the Book of Genesis are forbidden by God to eat from the tree of knowledge. Tempted by Satan they rebel. They become aware of their own sexuality, and are eventually banished from the Garden of Eden. Similarly, Victor's childhood is like paradise but he is seduced by knowledge in adulthood. He rebels by creating an unnatural man. The monster also becomes aware of his own 'fallen' state when he sees his own reflection.

Paradise Lost

Frankenstein and the monster share characteristics with God, Satan, Adam and Eve (see Summaries).

This is an **epic** (see Literary Terms) poem written by John Milton in the 1660s. It tells the story of how Satan was banished from heaven by God for leading a rebellion. Satan, unable to accept his fall into hell, decides to revenge himself by seducing Adam and Eve into evil and disobedience.

These references are sustained and add a whole new pattern of meaning to the novel.

PASSIONATE LITERATURE

The Romantics believed that nurture was to blame for man's evil, not nature, see p. 213.

Frankenstein is often seen as a **Romantic** (see Literary Terms) novel. Romanticism focuses on the expression of the imagination, exalted and intense feelings, visionary states of mind, and the **sublime** (see Literary Terms) power of nature. Romantics believed that art should have themes of great magnitude which could arouse emotional exhilaration in the audience.

The Romantics were influenced by philosophers of the **Enlightenment** (see Literary Terms), particularly those who either argued for individual liberty or explored the sublime.

An offshoot of **Romanticism** was the **Gothic novel** (see Literary Terms) which began in 1765 with Horace Walpole's dream-induced *The Castle of Otranto*. *Frankenstein* therefore belongs to the tradition of **fantasy** rather than **realism** (see Literary Terms). The **uncanny** events, stormy and dark **settings**, satanic **imagery** (see Literary Terms), and themes of revenge and pursuit are some of its Gothic features.

Secrets of science

Mary Shelley lived at a time of rapid progress in the sciences. One of the central preoccupations was the potential of electricity. In 1802 Galvani showed that running a current through the legs of frogs produced a twitch, and was thought to engender life. And, in 1803, Aldini attached a battery to the corpse of a criminal: 'The jaw of the deceased began to quiver, the adjoining muscles were horribly contorted, and one eye was actually opened … the right hand was raised and clenched, and the legs and thighs set in motion.'

Compare this description with the opening of Chapter 5.

These discoveries were discussed at Byron's villa. (Percy Shelley was known to have electrocuted himself until his hair stood on end and he possessed electro-magnetic kites which could bring down lightning in the event of a storm.)

PART TWO

SUMMARIES

GENERAL SUMMARY

Walton's story (Letters 1–4)

Young Captain Robert Walton is embarking upon a dangerous voyage to the North Pole, when he finds his ship surrounded by ice. While he is stuck, he sees the strange sight of a gigantic being on a dog-drawn sledge travelling at great speed who disappears into the fog. He then discovers Victor Frankenstein on the brink of death. Walton looks after him and they become friends, and Frankenstein tells him his story.

Victor's story (Chapters 1–10)

Victor, who came from a respectable Swiss family, grew up with an orphan named Elizabeth whom his mother had adopted. At seventeen, his mother died. At university he was inspired by a scientist called M. Waldman. Ambitious for glory, Victor learned everything he could about science in the hope that he could discover how to create life itself.

In a turmoil of obsession, he digs up corpses and builds a gigantic man from them in the hope of giving him life. He succeeds, but is devastated to find it so ugly, and runs away from it in horror. The monster disappears and Victor is nursed back to health by his friend Clerval.

However, he receives a letter from his father telling him that his youngest brother, William, has been murdered. Victor quickly journeys home to Geneva. On the way, he sees the monster amidst the Alps, and becomes convinced that the monster is William's murderer. When he meets his family, Victor learns that Justine Moritz, an honest servant of their family, has been accused of the murder. Victor is horrified but feels sure she will not be convicted. Justine's trial goes badly. She falsely confesses to the murder and is hanged. Unable to tell his family about the monster, Victor spends his time alone. On a mule he travels into the Alps where he meets the monster. He wants to kill him. The monster reproaches him and asks him to listen to his story.

The Monster's story (Chapters 11–16)

The monster tells him about the confusion of his early life. He could not distinguish anything but felt only pain, hunger and cold. Gradually, he learns about the world. On wandering into a village he is attacked by the villagers and flees into a hovel. In hiding he observes the daily life of a poor family called the De Laceys. He is moved by the kindness the son and daughter show towards their old, blind father. When a young Arabian arrives, the son teaches her his language and the monster decides to learn it by listening. Desperately needing friendship, the monster pins his hope on meeting the family. When the blind man is alone, he introduces himself. His conversation is interrupted by the return of the family. Seeing the monster clinging to his father, the son batters him. The family leave the cottage out of fear. In complete anguish, the monster decides to seek out his creator. On the way he saves a young girl from drowning but is shot by a peasant. Later, he sees a young boy, William, whom he wishes to befriend. William rejects him but also fatally reveals that he is a Frankenstein. In revenge for his miseries, the monster strangles him. He takes a portrait from his neck and places it within the dress of a girl who is sleeping – Justine. Finally, the monster explains that his misery and loneliness has made him act badly. He asks Victor to create a female monster for him.

Victor's story continues (Chapters 17–24)

Victor has many doubts but finally agrees to do so. When he returns home, his father proposes that Victor marry Elizabeth. Victor agrees to do so after he has taken a tour of England, on which he is accompanied by Clerval. Victor finally parts with his friend and hires a hut in the Orkney islands, so that he can make the female monster. But when he sees the monster at the window, in a fury, he tears the half-finished female creature to pieces. The monster, in despair, leaves him with the words, 'I will be with you on your wedding night!'

The monster murders Clerval out of revenge and makes it look as though Victor was the murderer. Victor spends time in prison in a state of madness. Eventually, he is proved innocent and is taken home by his father. He is married to Elizabeth, but, misinterpreting the monster's words, believes that the monster will kill him and decides to prepare for his own death. On their honeymoon, while Victor is out looking for the monster, he kills Elizabeth. Victor's father dies when he hears the news. Utterly alone, Victor decides to seek out the monster and kill him. He chases him across the globe and almost manages to kill him near the North Pole. Victor finds himself sinking when Walton's ship passes by and rescues him.

Walton's story continues (The final letters) Still stuck in ice, Walton's crew threaten to mutiny if he refuses to return. Victor gives them a rousing speech, urging them on. He finally dies from exhaustion. When Walton is writing his letters, he hears a noise and discovers the monster mourning the death of his creator. Walton calls him a hypocrite. Finally, the monster makes a long speech explaining how he has been mistreated and misunderstood by humanity. He declares that justice has never been given to him and the only solution is to commit suicide now his creator has gone. He jumps from the cabin window and 'is lost in darkness and distance'.

DETAILED SUMMARIES

CAPTAIN WALTON'S NARRATIVE (LETTERS 1–4)

LETTER 1
'A voyage of discovery to the land of knowledge'

Captain Walton is embarking on an ambitious expedition to the North Pole and is writing to reassure his sister Mrs Margaret Saville that his trip will be successful. He imagines that the Pole will be a beautiful region of 'light', is excited by the prospect that it is unknown and undiscovered, and hopes that he will be able to discover the secret of the magnet.

He reminisces on his early years which were spent passionately reading his uncle's collection of seafaring books. Against his father's dying wish, he spent six years training as a 'seafarer'.

COMMENT

We are introduced to the characteristics, values and desires of Robert Walton who is one of the main **narrators** (see Literary Terms, and Structure). His preoccupations reveal themes that are central to our understanding of the whole novel (see Themes). We see things from his perspective but we are also made to question his character.

Find other examples which show the strength of his imagination and his feelings.

Walton is a passionate, warm-hearted young man who is enthusiastic about his expedition. However, he might be led astray by the strength of his ambition and his longing for adventure. He has never been satisfied with what he has.

Walton's desire to turn 'the favourite dream of his early years' (p. 14) into a reality can be seen as either heroic or simply self-destructive. His 'ardent curiosity' to see the Pole 'is sufficient to conquer all fear and danger or death' (p. 14). As a child, his imagination was carried away by his uncle's books on voyaging which later led him to experience 'cold, famine, thirst and want of sleep' as a sailor (p. 15).

Similarly, his motives for going are **ambiguous** (see Literary Terms). Walton says he wants to 'benefit' mankind by his discoveries (p. 14) but also admits that he prefers 'glory' to 'ease and luxury' (p. 15).

Walton's language is eloquent and fluent but this is deceptive because his ideas are confused. He contradicts himself when he says that the 'cold breeze' gives him a 'foretaste' of the Pole's 'icy climes' but then claims that he doubts that the Pole is 'the seat of frost and desolation'. His strong imagination fantasises that 'snow and frost are banished' from the Pole. This is because the expedition was his 'favourite dream' as a child and explains why he *wants* to imagine the Pole as a beautiful place.

GLOSSARY   **Petersburgh** Russian capital (in the northwest)
the pole the North Pole was not discovered until 1909 by Robert Peary
wondrous power … needle why the needle of a compass is always attracted to the north
Homer the ancient Greek poet, who wrote *The Odyssey*, the heroic adventures of Odysseus beset with many dangers of the sea
Archangel a port in northeast Russia. This also alludes to Milton's archangels Satan and Gabriel in *Paradise Lost*

LETTER *2*   Three months have passed. Although Walton has found a ship and a crew, his 'enterprise' has been halted by bad weather.

Think whether Walton is aware of all his own weaknesses?

Walton feels gloomy and lonely because he needs a friend who could support him when there are difficulties.

He tells Margaret about two courageous members of his crew; the English lieutenant and the master.

Walton concludes that, even though he is despondent, he is still eager to start his exploration.

COMMENT   We are made to doubt Walton's vision in Letter 1 of the Pole as a region of 'eternal light' where 'the snow and frost are banished' (p. 13) because he has travelled further north to Archangel where he is surrounded by 'frost and snow' (p. 17). This **irony** (see Literary Terms) makes us criticise Walton's vivid imagination. He is an unreliable **narrator** (see Literary Terms).

Walton admits that Coleridge's imaginative poem caused his love for the ocean (pp. 19–20).

Observe how Walton confesses that he does not understand his own 'soul' (p. 20).

The importance of friendship is stressed because Walton's deep desire for a companion is in conflict with his desire to explore. He admits that his complaints are 'useless' because he is unlikely to find a friend on 'the wide ocean' (p. 18).

GLOSSARY

romantic the love of solitude expressed by some Romantic poets like Wordsworth, Byron and Shelley

feminine fosterage his sister Margaret was like a foster-mother to him when he was young

'Ancient Mariner' Samuel Taylor Coleridge's classic poem, 'The Rime of the Ancient Mariner' in which a seafarer introduces evil into the world out of ignorance by shooting an albatross

LETTER 3

Three more months have gone by. It is now summer and Walton is nearer the Pole. Although he is safe, his vessel is threatened by the dangers of the 'stiff gales' and 'floating sheets of ice'. Despite this, Walton is optimistic, the crew are courageous, and they wish to go on. Walton assures Margaret that he will be prudent, and shall avoid putting his crew at risk unnecessarily.

COMMENT

The images of warmth and cold, life and death are motifs in the novel.

We are made to question Walton's emotional stability. Optimistic in Letter 1, despondent in Letter 2, he is now again in 'good spirits'. It is unusual that the 'southern gales' give him a 'renovating warmth'.

Walton's desire both to succeed in his voyage and reassure Margaret leads him to contradict himself. His promise that he 'will be cool' and 'prudent' is broken by his heated and ambitious **rhetorical questions** (see Literary Terms) and exclamations at the end.

GLOSSARY **element** powers of nature, here referring to the ocean, wind and ice

LETTER 4

A month later (5 August), Walton's ship is stuck in the surrounding ice. The crew is distracted by the astonishing sight of a 'gigantic' man on a sledge vanishing into the distance. The following morning they discover another traveller. Although he is approaching death, he is hesitant to come aboard. Walton revives him with brandy. However, he shows feverish interest in Walton's sighting of the other traveller.

Walton's hope of finding a friend is fulfilled.

Note the ominous atmosphere.

Walton shares his ambitions with 'the stranger' (13 August) and his feelings for him grow into friendship. However, his friend is thrown into a wild despair when Walton confesses that he would sacrifice his own life in order to discover the knowledge which he desires.

Walton's curiosity is aroused (19 August) when the stranger wishes to tell him his life's history. He wants to warn Walton that an extreme desire for knowledge can be dangerous and hopes that Walton will be able to see a clear moral in the story he is about to tell. Walton resolves to record the story faithfully and send the manuscript to Margaret.

COMMENT The remoteness of the **setting** prepares us for the strange sighting of the two travellers and the fantastic tale that Frankenstein intends to tell. The Pole's **sublimity** (see Literary Terms) is suggested by the untamed wildness of the icy landscape.

These letters set up a contrast between the two travellers. The creature is seen as 'gigantic', 'savage' and belonging to 'some undiscovered land'. He is strange, different and unknown, whereas Frankenstein is an *Darkness and* 'attractive and 'amiable' (p. 26) 'European' who can *light are* speak 'English' (p. 24). However, there is a tension *prevailing motifs* between the light and dark aspects of Frankenstein's *in the novel; look* character: he has a 'double existence'. His emaciation *for examples so* and 'madness' can be lit up with 'a beam of benevolence' *far.* (p. 25).

Note any other The seduction of knowledge emerges as the crucial *references to* theme of the whole novel. Frankenstein thinks Walton *knowledge.* is like him because he is 'pursuing the same course' (p. 28). He sees it as his duty as a friend to warn Walton of the harm that knowledge can do; without friends, humans are only 'half made-up' (p. 27).

GLOSSARY **celestial spirit** heavenly spirit
animated brought life and movement into
unfashioned not completely made

A *Identify the speaker.*

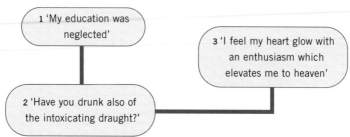

1 'My education was neglected'

2 'Have you drunk also of the intoxicating draught?'

3 'I feel my heart glow with an enthusiasm which elevates me to heaven'

Identify the person 'to whom' this comment refers.

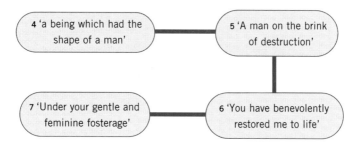

4 'a being which had the shape of a man'

5 'A man on the brink of destruction'

7 'Under your gentle and feminine fosterage'

6 'You have benevolently restored me to life'

Check your answers on page 96.

B *Consider these issues.*

a What is revealed of Walton as a character and what Shelley makes you think of him.

b Your opening impressions of Victor.

c How Shelley creates an **atmosphere** (see Literary Terms) of tension, strangeness and uncertainty in Letter 4.

d Your expectations as a reader concerning Walton's ambition for knowledge.

e Shelley's use of emotional language to explore the state of mind of her characters.

f How Shelley shows Walton's isolation and loneliness.

VICTOR FRANKENSTEIN'S NARRATIVE (CHAPTERS 1–5)

CHAPTER 1
'The beauty of the dream vanished'

Victor tells his tale over the course of one week: 20–26 August.

Victor Frankenstein begins his tale with his family history. He was born into a wealthy Swiss family famous for its involvement in law and politics. His father, Alphonse Frankenstein, had married Caroline Beaufort. She had been left an orphan when her father, previously a rich merchant and Alphonse's best friend, lost his wealth, became a recluse and died. Victor was born on their travels in Italy.

He had a happy childhood and grew up with his foster-sister, Elizabeth. She was an orphan who had been rescued from a poor peasant family by Caroline.

COMMENT

Victor Frankenstein is the main **narrator** (see Literary Terms) of the novel. He tells Walton his version of events in the first person. Walton writes down what Victor tells him. His wish to reveal the cause of his misfortunes, which he had originally intended to keep secret, gives the story a personal and intimate feeling.

Victor is also the central character of his own story. His beliefs, passions and ways of judging other people and himself make a crucial contribution to the novel's meaning. This emphasises that *how* a story is told is as important as *what* is told.

Recall that Margaret acts as a foster-parent to her brother Walton (p. 18).

This chapter introduces the reader to the importance Victor places upon the role of parents. He sees Caroline and Alphonse as responsible parents who 'fulfilled their duties' (p. 32) towards him. His happy childhood is entirely due to their 'stores of affection' and kindness.

Caroline emerges as a gentle and loving character. The heavenly language Victor uses to describe her suggests her goodness and virtue. She acts as a 'guardian angel' to Elizabeth. These qualities are echoed in Elizabeth who 'bears a celestial stamp in all her features' (p. 33).

VICTOR FRANKENSTEIN'S NARRATIVE

Shelley uses minor characters here to help the reader judge the central characters. The two **Romantic** (see Literary Terms) stories which relate the histories of Caroline and Elizabeth reveal a contrast between male and female attitudes.

Find similarities between Walton and these male characters.

Beaufort and Elizabeth's real parent, 'the Milanese nobleman', are seen as irresponsible fathers who unnecessarily plunge their own daughters into distress. Beaufort forces Caroline to live with him in a wretched isolation out of honour and 'false pride' (p. 30). Elizabeth's father is inspired by the 'antique glory' of Italy and leaves her behind in order to fight for his country.

GLOSSARY   **syndics** chief magistrate. Geneva was governed by four of these because it was a republic

CHAPTER *2*

Recall how Walton's fascination for the sea was inspired by 'Uncle Thomas's books' and 'The Ancient Mariner' (pp. 17–19).

Victor explains that, from an early age, Elizabeth loved nature and poetry but he yearned to discover explanations for the world around him. His early imagination was inspired by a book by Cornelius Agrippa, and by what Agrippa wanted to find: immortality, eternal youth, and the power to raise the dead. Victor feels that these events determine his destiny. Two years later, when a thunderbolt burned a tree to a stump, Victor felt that nature was so mysterious that science would never be able to explain the causes of things and he gave up his studies. However, his destiny to be a scientist could not be avoided.

COMMENT   This chapter shifts the focus to Victor himself who describes his character as a youth.

It is questionable whether Victor really learned self-control (p. 32).

Note important differences between the characters of Elizabeth and Victor: she is calm, gentle and passive, whereas his 'violent' temper and 'eager desire to learn' would have made him 'sullen' without her influence.

This characterisation prepares us for Victor's behaviour in Chapter 4 when he is away from Elizabeth.

Recall the danger of Walton's ambitions on p. 27.

Victor's admiration for his friend, Henry Clerval, reveals his own ambitious desire (p. 39). Clerval emerges as an imaginative and adventurous character who dreams of being famous. This extends the catalogue of dissatisfied male characters who are unable to let things be.

Note the mysterious attraction of science: nature's laws are 'secrets' that are 'hidden' (p. 36).

Collect evidence which reveals Victor's wildness.

The reader feels a sense of foreboding each time Victor reminds Walton that he has been ruined. He suggests that he has become the victim of his own passion. His 'thirst for knowledge' (p. 35) 'ruled' his 'fate' which led to his 'destruction' (p. 40).

The dangers of a strong imagination are signalled. His youthful 'bright visions' of success are contrasted with his later 'gloomy' condition (p. 37).

GLOSSARY

wandering life much of Mary Shelley's life with Percy was spent travelling Italy, Germany and Switzerland

Natural philosophy science, which in the eighteenth century referred to all branches of human knowledge

Cornelius Agrippa German scholar (1486–1535) reputed to have raised spirits from the dead, and author of *De Occulta Philosophia* and *On the Vanity of all Human Knowledge*

Paracelsus Swiss physician and alchemist (1493?–1541)

Albertus Magnus philosopher (1193 or 1206–1280), known as the Universal Doctor

the philosopher's stone and the elixir of life alchemists looked for these, the first was thought to be able to change base metals into gold, and the second was thought to give eternal life

galvanism Luigi Galvani (1737–98) believed that electricity was to be found in the joints and muscles of animals

CHAPTER 3   At seventeen, Victor's departure for the University of Ingolstadt is delayed by the death of his mother who, in looking after Elizabeth's fever, came down with it herself. Victor's spirits rise when he considers what knowledge university would bring. On arrival at Ingolstadt, Victor meets two professors. He dislikes M. Krempe's brusque manner and the way he scorns his enthusiasm for alchemy. Victor, however, is not persuaded by Krempe's belief in the virtues of modern science. Despite this, he is overcome with inspiration by the other professor, M. Waldman, a chemist, who gives a rousing speech on the brilliance of modern science.

COMMENT

This chapter begins a tension in Victor's priorities.

There is a conflict between Victor's studies and his relationships with others. He feels deep grief over his mother's death and sadness at having to leave his family to go to university. However, his gloomy loneliness is relieved by the prospect of acquiring knowledge.

Observe how Victor's enthusiasm for study develops into an obsession in Chapters 3–4.

Victor is portrayed as an anti-social man who dislikes meeting strangers. He often judges people by their physical appearance. This is seen in his contempt for M. Krempe and his respect for M. Waldman.

Waldman's declaration that only modern scientists have 'performed miracles' persuades Victor to abandon alchemy (p. 46).

Waldman's lecture were the 'words of fate enounced to destroy me' (p. 46).

Notice the climax in Shelley's writing when she depicts Victor's emotional response to Waldman's lecture. His desire to 'explore unknown powers' creates inner 'turmoil' (p. 46).

GLOSSARY

Ingolstadt in Germany. During the mid eighteenth century a secret society of believers in republicanism, the Illuminati, met at the University there

'old familiar faces' a poem by Charles Lamb (1775–1834), one of the many writers who visited Godwin's house

CHAPTER 4   Victor becomes obsessed with his scientific studies, and fails to visit his family for two years. Possessed by an ambition to discover the cause of life, he frantically digs up dead bodies from graveyards so that he can experiment upon them. Finally, he finds a way to give life to dead matter.

His studies are destructive to himself and his relationships with others.

Astonished by his success, Victor goes a step further and stitches together a colossal man from the limbs of corpses whom he hopes to give life. Despite the beautiful spring and a worried letter from Alphonse, Victor is unable to tear himself away from his midnight labours.

COMMENT   The **Gothic settings** (see Literary Terms)of the graves, churchyards, and dissecting-rooms evoke an eerie atmosphere.

Victor's language is very descriptive.

His 'workshop of filthy creation' and his 'profane fingers' are details that suggest Victor now thinks his experiments were morally wrong (p. 52).

Victor is at pains to show that he could not control himself. He appears possessed by an almighty force. He fixes his sights upon 'one object of pursuit' (p. 49) which takes an 'irresistible hold' of him (p. 53).

VICTOR FRANKENSTEIN'S NARRATIVE

Remember
Elizabeth's
contentment with
the 'appearances of
things' (p. 35).

Victor's isolation from society is clearly shown as a consequence of his obsession for scientific discovery. It emaciates him, makes him oblivious to daytime and the beauty of nature, and causes him to forget his friends and family.

Imagination is
associated with
brightness and
reality with
darkness.

There is a growing distinction between the inner world of the imagination and the outer world of reality. Victor is not repelled by his experiments because he feels that if he discovered a way to create life then mankind would 'bless' him for conquering death (p. 51).

GLOSSARY

charnel-houses houses for dead bodies

the Arabian Sinbad is buried alive with the corpse of his wife but finds the distant light of a passage through which he escapes

CHAPTER 5

Notice how the
opening
description triggers
the reader's
imagination.

On a 'dreary' night, Victor waits apprehensively for the body to come alive. The body shudders. The corpse breathes. Victor is filled with horror and rushes out of the room. He goes to bed, hoping to forget what he has done, but is disturbed by a nightmare about Elizabeth. He wakes but the monster is next to his bed, staring at him. Victor escapes again and passes the night and morning alone and tormented. Walking aimlessly, he bumps into his friend Clerval. Victor takes him back home and is wild with delight to find the monster has gone. His mad laughter and feverish behaviour frighten Clerval who has to look after him for five months.

COMMENT

This chapter is a turning point in Victor's life. The reversal of his fortune is shown clearly. Victor's disappointment in his experiment is shown by his despair, disbelief and horror at the creature's ugliness. Victor sees the consequences of his actions for the first time.

Victor's childlike behaviour implies an inability to recognise his responsibilities. He abandons the creature twice and dreads its presence when he returns to his study.

This is a key theme.

Ironically (see Literary Terms), Victor fails to experience the sense of duty towards his creation that his own parents had felt for him.

Reconsider this dream as the novel progresses.

Victor's dream hints at his underlying guilt. When he kisses Elizabeth she transforms into Caroline's corpse: **symbolising** (see Literary Terms) that Victor's desires will bring destruction.

Friendship is an important motif in the book.

Clerval's appearance emphasises the importance Shelley attaches to friendships. Victor feels a 'calm and serene joy' (p. 58) on seeing him, a feeling that contrasts with the enthusiastic frenzy of his experiments.

GLOSSARY   **Dante** Italian poet (1265–1321) who wrote *The Inferno* which describes the tortures of hell

Like one, that … tread from Coleridge's poem 'The Rime of the Ancient Mariner'

the Dutch schoolmaster in Oliver Goldsmith's (1730–74) novel believes that there is little use in knowing Greek

A *Identify the speaker.*

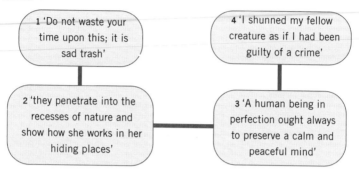

1 'Do not waste your time upon this; it is sad trash'

4 'I shunned my fellow creature as if I had been guilty of a crime'

2 'they penetrate into the recesses of nature and show how she works in her hiding places'

3 'A human being in perfection ought always to preserve a calm and peaceful mind'

Identify the person 'to whom' this comment refers.

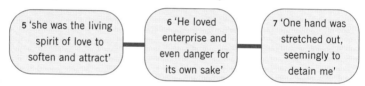

5 'she was the living spirit of love to soften and attract'

6 'He loved enterprise and even danger for its own sake'

7 'One hand was stretched out, seemingly to detain me'

Check your answers on page 96.

 B *Consider these issues.*

a How Shelley develops the relationship between Victor and his studies.

b How Victor creates a sense of foreboding in the reader.

c How Shelley reveals differences between Victor's childhood and his later years.

d The similarities and differences between Walton and Victor.

e The similarities and differences between male and female characters.

f The impact that imagination and passion play in the development of Victor's character.

g How Shelley evokes a dark atmosphere in the descriptions of Victor's pursuits.

h The portrayal of the monster as a fearful being.

VICTOR'S NARRATIVE CONTINUES (CHAPTERS 6–10)

CHAPTER 6
'Cursed by the hands that formed you'

A letter from Elizabeth asks Victor to write home; Geneva is still the beautiful place it was in their childhood; little has changed. She explains that a servant girl, Justine Moritz, came back to their family after her mother died. Finally she describes the growth of Ernest, now sixteen, and William, Victor's younger brothers.

Victor tries to forget his creation.

Victor replies but delays his return. Remaining at Ingolstadt, he introduces Clerval to his professors. He develops a dislike for science and turns to oriental languages. Time passes and Victor feels increasingly cheerful and back to his old self. Before he goes home, he takes a short tour of the countryside with Clerval.

COMMENT

The stable, cheerful, and outdoor life of Victor's family contrasts with the change in Victor's health.

Elizabeth is a parallel with Margaret.

Elizabeth has replaced Caroline in the role of mother, implied by the way she refers to Victor's brothers as 'our dear children'.

The relationship between Justine and her mother prefigures the relationship that will develop between the monster and Victor. Victor will feel guilty for his cruelty to the monster but will also blame him as the cause for his family's misery.

Victor's decision to keep the monster an unspeakable secret causes an inner conflict, a tension that becomes more acute in the following chapters. His continual delays in returning home suggests a deep-rooted guilt.

Consider whether Victor's claim that he loved 'nature' is convincing.

Shelley uses **irony** (see Literary Terms) to criticise Victor's behaviour. It is ironic that he is tormented by the praise Waldman and Krempe give him. It is also ironic that he realises his experiments were a 'selfish pursuit' (p. 67) but fails to acknowledge that his attempt to forget the creature by pursuing other interests is equally selfish.

GLOSSARY   **Angelica** heroine of Ariosto's (1474–1535) *Orlando Furioso*

CHAPTER 7   On returning from his tour, Victor learns in a letter from his father that his youngest brother William has been strangled. In despair, he leaves immediately for Geneva but arrives late. The city gates are shut. Taking a different route across the mountains, he is shocked to see the monster, who is suddenly lit up by lightning.

Do you think Victor is justified in his suspicions?   The monster disappears. Victor immediately believes that it is the guilty murderer of William.

At daybreak, Victor enters Geneva. He decides not to tell the authorities to chase the monster because they would probably not believe his story and think he was mad. When he arrives home, Ernest tells him that the murderer is their servant, Justine, but Victor is convinced of her innocence.

COMMENT   The cheerful tone at the end of Chapter 6 is quickly reversed by the news of William's murder. The theme of crime is introduced. The missing portrait of Caroline becomes an important piece of evidence in Chapters 8 and 16.

This motif emphasises Victor's desire to forget his horrors.   Shelley asks us to connect two incidents by the use of a **motif** (see Literary Terms). Victor covers his face with his hands when he reads the letter. This recalls his reaction (p. 59) when he imagines that the monster is in his apartment. Victor's inability to accept the monster may have disastrous consequences.

Shelley revels in describing images of **sublime** (see Literary Terms) nature: thunder, lightning and the vast mountains create a tense, uncertain atmosphere.

Victor's description of the monster as a 'wretch' and 'filthy daemon' (p. 73) affects the reader's perception.

The **uncanny** (see Literary Terms) appearance of the monster immediately after Victor's lament for William makes us associate the monster with dark and evil forces.

There is conflict when Victor hears that Justine has been accused, whereas he feels that the monster is the real culprit. The reader knows, however, that Victor's evidence would not stand up in court.

GLOSSARY

the palaces of nature from Lord Byron's poem *Childe Harold's Pilgrimage*, Canto III, 590–4

CHAPTER 8

While Victor awaits Justine's trial, he blames himself for William's death. Although Justine appears calm and innocent, the case against her is strong. The public become suspicious. In her defence, she explains all the circumstances apart from one crucial piece of evidence: how she came to be wearing the portrait of Caroline. Elizabeth makes a speech defending Justine but it backfires.

When, after a sleepless night, Victor returns to court he is astonished to find that Justine has confessed her guilt. Elizabeth and Victor visit her in prison, only to discover that the priest bullied her into confessing a lie. Justine is hanged.

COMMENT

Consider whether a monster is a symbol of those mistreated by society.

Shelley introduces a crucial theme: the political theme of justice. She shows the unfairness of the legal system and reveals corruption in religious institutions. The 'mockery of justice' (p. 78) is seen by the way the judges prejudge Justine as guilty. It is a macabre **irony** (see Literary Terms) that a man of God should cruelly abuse his power and force Justine to confess a lie. Notice how he makes her feel like a 'monster' (p. 83).

The crowd is portrayed as fickle. Their mean-minded prejudice is shown when they use Justine as a scapegoat for their anger.

Note further contrasts between good and evil language as the book progresses.

The religious and legal language points out a contrast between the virtuous Justine and the immoral Victor: Justine, 'a saintly sufferer' (p. 85) becomes the second 'victim' to Victor's 'unhallowed arts' and 'lawless devices'. Victor confesses himself as the 'true murderer' (p. 84).

CHAPTER 9

Feeling responsible for the deaths of two innocent people, Victor wallows in solitude and gloom. His inner thoughts turn to revenge. Alphonse and Elizabeth are worried about him. The family retire to their other home at Belrive where Victor seeks relief from his feelings by journeying through the astounding scenery of the Alps.

COMMENT

The way Victor contradicts himself reveals his difficulty in coming to terms with the deaths of William and Justine. Victor confesses that he 'not in deed, but in effect, was the true murderer' (p. 89) but also wishes to revenge the 'crimes and malice' of the monster (p. 88).

Find evidence to suggest that Victor is as monstrous as the monster.

Victor's wish to kill the monster gives Elizabeth's comment a dark **irony** (see Literary Terms): 'Men appear to me as monsters thirsting for each other's blood' (p. 88).

Shelley uses satanic language to underscore Victor's fall in into despair. He wanders like an 'evil spirit' who feels a 'hell of intense tortures' (p. 86).

Now Victor's secret has affected the lives of others, he becomes even guiltier and more isolated. However, we feel that his 'deep, dark, deathlike solitude' will not solve any problems (p. 86).

CHAPTER 10

Scaling a mountain of vast irregular beauty, Victor gazes at the desolate 'sea of ice'. In the mist, bounding towards him at frightening speed, is his creation. They speak to each other for the first time. Victor, accusing him of murder and wanting revenge for William's death, tries to kill him. The monster avoids his attack and pleads with Victor to listen to him. He explains how he has suffered because Victor abandoned him. He begs Victor for sympathy and implores him to listen to his tale. Victor agrees and they find shelter in a lonely hut. The monster begins his tale.

COMMENT   Notice Shelley's portrayal of nature as a grand, awesome and destructive power. The 'broken' and 'bent' trees, the 'jutting rocks', and the 'traces' of the 'avalanche' reflect the 'wreck' that Victor has become mentally and physically (p. 93).

The return of the monster is an important motif

It is **ironic** (see Literary Terms) that the monster chooses the moment to appear when Victor is feeling sorry for himself and about to 'forget the passing cares' (p. 93) of life. This illustrates Victor's self-deception.

The monster does hint that he is 'guilty' (p. 96).

There are a number of surprises for the reader when we meet the monster. First, he does not seem to be a monster at all but a 'creature' with very human and sensitive feelings. We feel sorry for his loneliness and admiration for his intelligence. Secondly, it is

'You accuse me of murder, and yet you would, with a satisfied conscience, destroy your own creature' (p. 96).

unexpected when the political concerns of Chapter 8 re-emerge in the monster's speeches. He demands 'justice', 'duty', and 'affection' from Victor (p. 96). His abandonment stresses Victor's responsibility towards him. Finally, when the monster points out Victor's hypocrisy we are given an important new viewpoint of Victor's actions. The reader is made more critical of Victor's perception of things.

The monster's story is told in the barren, desolate and remote scene of the 'sea of ice' near the top of a mountain. This link to the setting behind Victor's tale, the North Pole, emphasises the isolation and doom of both these characters.

GLOSSARY   **We rest** from Percy Shelley's poem, 'Mutability'

Identify the speaker.

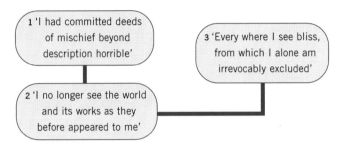

1 'I had committed deeds of mischief beyond description horrible'

2 'I no longer see the world and its works as they before appeared to me'

3 'Every where I see bliss, from which I alone am irrevocably excluded'

Identify the person 'to whom' this comment refers.

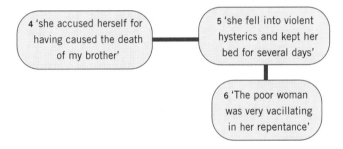

4 'she accused herself for having caused the death of my brother'

5 'she fell into violent hysterics and kept her bed for several days'

6 'The poor woman was very vacillating in her repentance'

Check your answers on page 96.

 Consider these issues.

a Victor's troubled conscience with regard to his past actions.

b The growth and causes of Victor's isolation.

c The nature and development of Victor's relationships with his family.

d The presentation and effect of nature on the characters.

e The rhythms of the novel so far: what are the moments of high tension?

f How the theme of justice is developed and depicted.

g The role of secrecy so far.

THE MONSTER'S NARRATIVE (CHAPTERS 11–16)

CHAPTER 11

'I gazed with a kind of wonder'

The monster's early life is crowded with confusion. He feels raw sensations but is unable to understand them or the world around him. He finds shelter in the forest and sleeps. He wakes in the night. Cold, frightened and alone, he cries. The first object he can make out is the moon and he is enchanted by it.

This begins an important association of the monster with night; re-read p. 56.

Gradually, the monster learns to distinguish between his senses. He starts to learn about the world by trial and error. He discovers the cause behind fire and tries to cook his food.

He enters a hut and an old man flees. He eats the man's dinner. Roaming across the fields, he reaches a village but the villagers brutally attack him. He flees and finds shelter in a hovel, attached to a cottage. He sees a young woman, a young man and an old man. He observes their actions but does not understand what they mean.

COMMENT

The monster takes up the story, becoming the third main **narrator** (see Literary Terms). Victor tells Walton what the monster told him. The monster's character, attitudes and ways of judging people make a crucial contribution to the novel as a whole.

The monster is a benign being.

The enchantment he feels for the world around him reveals his true nature. His innocence is seen in the simplicity of his language and actions. His description of the birds as 'little winged animals' has a child-like quality. Although it is wrong for him to enter the old man's cottage and steal his food, he is unaware of this and means no harm.

The monster's pity for the De Lacey's reflects our pity for the monster.

His pleasure at hearing De Lacey's music, and his sorrow at the family's distress reveal him to be a creature of beautiful feelings and natural sympathies.

Our sympathies completely shift from Victor to the monster. Although Victor is a victim of the monster, the monster is clearly a victim of society and his own abandonment. His pain at being attacked by the villagers and his lack of understanding of the situation stress his vulnerability.

Notice how the obscurity of the language in the opening illustrates the confusion of his first experiences.

GLOSSARY   **a multiplicity of sensations** the philosopher John Locke believed that the human mind, at birth, is like a blank sheet. Knowledge is learned from pure sensation. We can see the monster learning from trial and error

Pandaemonium chaos. In Milton's *Paradise Lost*, the devils, having been thrown out of heaven, retire to Pandemonium to plot against God. This reference is clearly **ironic** (see Literary Terms)

the barbarity of man Jean-Jacques Rousseau asserted that man is born naturally benign but society corrupts him. The contrast between the monster's harmlessness and man's cruelty confirms this

CHAPTER 12

How do you respond to the monster's feelings?

The monster continues to watch the family in the cottage, trying to work out the reasons behind their behaviour. He is moved by the kindness that the young man and woman show towards the old blind man. He likes the family but is too frightened to join them. When he finds out that their sadness is caused by poverty, he collects firewood for them in the night.

He discovers that they use language to communicate their thoughts and feelings. He passionately desires to learn language and starts to pick up the basics,

This is a symbolic moment of self-discovery.

hoping that one day he will be able to speak to the cottagers.

Admiring the beauty of the family, the monster is mortified when he sees his own reflection in a pool.

COMMENT

Can you find evidence suggesting the monster has a strong imagination?

This chapter focuses on the monster's learning and his need to explain the world around him.

Notice how the language creates an **ironic** (see Literary Terms) parallel between the monster and Victor. We see scientific language in his wish to 'discover' the 'cause' behind the De Lacey's unhappiness. Furthermore, his ambitions are emotionally charged for he 'ardently desired' and 'eagerly longed' to befriend the De Laceys. Unlike Victor, his attention and hopes are fixed on other human beings.

Friendly and virtuous actions come naturally to the monster. When he finds out that the De Laceys are poverty-stricken, he acts upon his knowledge by collecting firewood for them.

GLOSSARY

The ass and the lap-dog from La Fontaine's *Fables*. The ass copies the fawning of the dog but gets beaten instead of stroked by its master

CHAPTER 13

In spring a beautiful woman arrives, an Arabian called Safie. Felix is overjoyed to see her and starts to teach her their language by reading from a history book called *Ruins of Empires*. The monster finds this an ideal opportunity to acquire language by listening from his hovel. Within two months he is able to understand everyday conversations. However, he learns things about mankind from *Ruins of Empires* which shock and disgust him. He is upset by the tales of war, injustice and abuse of power. Despite this, he is more pained when he learns about birth, children and families because this leads him to question his own origin, parentage and present isolation.

Recall the fate of Justin.

COMMENT

This chapter is about the forces which shape the monster's personality. Like Victor, books are an important influence. Knowledge has a powerful effect on him. The more he learns about society, the less he seems to know about himself. He realises that he has no money, property, family, or friends. His question, 'What was I' (p. 117), shows a growing self-awareness of his own difference.

Consider the relevance that 'knowledge clings to the mind' (p. 116).

His natural goodness is shown by the way he turns away with 'disgust' at the deeds of 'bloodshed' described in *Ruins of Empires*.

The character of Safie is important because the De Laceys welcome her into their family, despite the difference of her appearance and culture. This contrasts with the rejection that the monster has experienced so far.

We see the emergence of the monster's sexual feelings. Although Agatha 'enticed' his 'love' (p. 103), he is separated by his ugliness. This contrasts with Felix who has a female companion in Safie.

GLOSSARY   **Ruins of Empires** by Comte de Volney (1791)

CHAPTER 14

The monster is moved by the life story of the De Laceys. He discovers that they were a wealthy French family who had their wealth confiscated by the authorities because Felix had helped a Turkish merchant to escape from prison. He had been horrified when the French law had unfairly condemned the Turk to death. As a reward the Turk promised Felix his daughter, Safie's hand in marriage. They fell in love but Felix had to return to Paris because De Lacey and Agatha had been imprisoned for their involvement in the escape. They were all banished from France. Above this, Safie's father did not want to honour his promise to Felix. Safie, however, ran away from her father and found the De Laceys.

The letters between Felix and Sofie convince Walton of Victor's tale (p. 202).

COMMENT   At the centre of the book is another story. It is significant because it reveals more about the major characters and it develops the themes (see Literary Terms). However, the story links to events that will happen in the book as well as events that have already happened.

- The Turk's promise to reward Felix with his daughter, Safie and the subsequent breaking of the promise mirrors Victor's vacillation over creating a female mate for the monster (Chapters 17, 18 and 20).
- The Turk's 'tyrannical' (p. 122) mistreatment of Safie mirrors Victor's stubborn cruelty towards his child – the creature (Chapters 10 and 20).
- The Turk's ingratitude towards Felix is due to his religious differences. His prejudices reflect the misplaced hatred Victor and the whole of society have towards the creature.
- Like Victor, Felix's ambitions and reckless actions cause the plight of his family. (Chapters 7, 8, 21–23). However, Felix battles for justice and freedom whereas Victor imprisons the creature in isolation

by his final refusal to complete his female mate
(Chapter 20).

- Persecution of the Turk by the French authorities
reveals the corruption of the law. This injustice
reflects Justine's mistreatment in Chapter 8.

CHAPTER 15

The monster learned to love virtue and hate vice from
the story of the De Laceys. However, he experienced
much more complex and advanced feelings when he
read three books which he found by chance. *The*
Other characters,   *Sorrows of Young Werther* made him feel both joyous and
too, are affected by   sad. Plutarch's *Lives* helped him admire heroic leaders
books.   and despise tyrants. In contrast, *Paradise Lost* makes
him identify his lonely state with Satan's banishment
from heaven. Sometimes he became envious of the
beautiful home of the De Laceys. When he discovers
Victor's journal, which records how he was made, he is
disgusted.

One hope keeps him alive: the belief that the De
Laceys will overlook his deformity and accept his
friendship. He reveals himself to the blind old man
when the others are out. When they return, the
monster clings to De Lacey in fright. He is violently
beaten by Felix, and flees in despair.

COMMENT   This chapter marks an abrupt change in the hopes,
feelings and natural goodness of the monster. He
portrays the agony of his desolation by comparing
himself to Satan. Satan's rebellion against God is
similar to the way the monster curses his creator upon
finding the journal. The hellish isolation of his hovel
compared to the 'bliss' (p. 125) of the cottagers'
paradise makes him envious.

The monster's decision to meet the blind old man alone
inspires hope. The tone of calm sorrow of their

conversation and the open-minded sympathy of De Lacey towards the friendless monster contrasts with the scene of brutal violence which follows. This shock emphasises the creature's reversal in fortune.

Notice the importance of viewpoint (see Themes). Felix misinterprets the creature's fearful clinging as an attack upon his father.

GLOSSARY   **The path of my departure was free** slightly misquoted from Percy Shelley's poem, 'Mutability'

The Sorrows of Werter by the German **Romantic** (see Literary Terms) Goethe (1749–1832). The hero of the novel finally commits suicide when his love is unrequited by a married woman. Like *Frankenstein*, this novel is written in the style of a confession

Lives by Plutarch (119–46BC). This ancient Roman author wrote biographies of the great Greek and Roman leaders. The law-givers who are mentioned were all Athenian statesmen

Paradise Lost epic poem by John Milton (1608–74), which explores the banishment of Satan from heaven, and Satan's plot to revenge this by corrupting mankind. Written in a **sublime** (see Literary Terms) style, Milton became a hero for the **Romantic** writers

Adam's supplication in *Paradise Lost* Adam asks God for a female companion in Book 8.357–97. Unlike Victor, Adam's creator carries out his wishes

CHAPTER 16

Finding his only bond to mankind broken, the monster is reduced to despair. He reflects that he revealed himself to De Lacey too hastily and he resolves to talk with him again. He is frightened when the family does not reappear. Felix returns and tells the landlord that they are leaving. Lonely and dejected, the monster releases his fury by burning the cottage.

The evidence used to convict Justine is finally explained.

He decides to seek out his creator. On the way, he saves a young girl from drowning but a man shoots him. After two months, he arrives at Geneva and finds a young child whom he wishes to befriend. When the child reveals that he is a Frankenstein, the monster strangles him. He takes a miniature portrait from the child's body. When he finds a barn to hide in he sees a young girl sleeping. He is attracted to her but this makes him feel even more isolated and frustrated. In revenge, he places the portrait on her dress.

Finally, he asks Frankenstein to create an ugly female companion for him.

COMMENT

This chapter shows how the monster's exclusion by the De Laceys changes his character and destiny.

The mood darkens with the deepening comparisons to Satan. The monster is portrayed as beast-like, powerful and destructive. Although he declares 'an everlasting war against mankind' (p. 131) in revenge, he also seeks 'justice' from Victor (p. 134).

The theme of prejudice is developed by the way William and the peasant misunderstand the monster's actions and intentions.

Do you think the monster's violence is justified?

The monster's frustrated revenge will become tragic. The murdering of William and the framing of Justine make Victor mistrust him.

The sexual feelings the monster has towards Justine explain his demands for a female companion.

The monster's account finally unravels the mystery behind Caroline's portrait in Chapter 8.

GLOSSARY

I bore a hell within me recalls *Paradise Lost* when Satan says, 'Which way I fly is hell, myself am Hell' in Book 4.75
with the world before me recalls the ending of *Paradise Lost* when the world was before Adam and Eve as they made their way out of the Garden of Eden

 **A** *Identify the speaker.*

1 'My virtues will necessarily arise when I live in communion with an equal'

2 'there is something in your words that persuades me you are sincere'

Identify the person 'to whom' this comment refers.

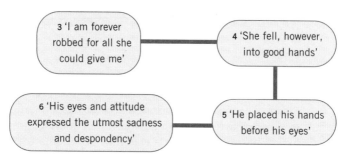

3 'I am forever robbed for all she could give me'

4 'She fell, however, into good hands'

6 'His eyes and attitude expressed the utmost sadness and despondency'

5 'He placed his hands before his eyes'

Check your answers on page 96.

 B *Consider these issues.*

a Your impressions of the monster. Whether Victor's description of him as a 'vile insect' sums him up.

b Similarities and differences between Victor, Walton and the monster.

c Similarities and differences between the monster and the female characters so far.

d The portrayal of the monster as a harmless being.

e The effect that knowledge and reading has on the monster, Clerval, Walton and Victor.

f The emotional nature of the monster's reactions to the De Laceys.

g The contradictions within the monster's personality.

h The reasons why Safie is accepted by the De Laceys but the monster is not.

i Whether the monster's rejection by the De Laceys justifies his revenge.

VICTOR'S SECOND NARRATIVE (CHAPTERS 17-24)

CHAPTER 17
'I will be with you on your wedding night'

The monster again asks Victor to create a female companion for him. Victor refuses, enraged by the monster's account of William's murder. The monster asks for sympathy and promises to live away from mankind, in peace, if Victor grants his wish. Victor is moved and changes his mind: he is persuaded that a female companion would stop the creature's misery and therefore remove the cause behind his crimes. The monster promises to reappear when Victor has created his mate. He leaves. In the dark Victor makes his way back to Chamonix but feels depressed by his promise.

Find examples of Victor's ambivalence (see Literary Terms) throughout this chapter.

COMMENT

Victor takes over the narrative for the second time. The form of spoken dialogue used in this chapter gives the reader a sense of immediacy and conflict.

Victor is persuaded to make the female because:
- He fears the monster's power: 'I will revenge my injuries, if I cannot inspire love, I will cause fear.' Victor agrees 'to save' his family (p. 144).
- The monster is prepared to make sacrifices, promising to live with his mate 'cut off from the world' (p. 141).
- Victor feels guilty for abandoning the monster who explains that his crimes are due to a 'forced solitude' (p. 142).
- He is moved by the monster's pain and wishes to 'console him' (p. 142).
- He realises it is his moral duty. The creature demands the female 'as a right' (p. 140). Victor concludes it would be 'justice to him and my fellow creatures' to comply.
- He is aware that the monster began life as a naturally good being.

Do you think Victor is to be blamed for William's murder?

Notice that Victor has doubts:

- If he makes another creature, then together they could cause even more destruction.
- They will not be able to keep themselves in exile, admiring the superior qualities of man.

These concerns sow the seeds of Victor's inner conflict, self-doubt and misery.

CHAPTER 18

Victor puts off his work, disgusted by the thought of creating another monster. Alphonse, however, thinks that Victor's gloom is because he is secretly in love with another woman. Alphonse questions him about his depression but Victor assures him that he loves Elizabeth. Alphonse is delighted and suggests immediate marriage. However, Victor puts it off, suggesting that a journey to England would solve his gloom. Secretly, Alphonse arranges for Clerval to join Victor on his trip. This thwarts Victor's plans to create a new monster in secrecy. As they travel through Europe, Clerval enjoys the beautiful scenery but Victor cannot stop thinking about his promise to the monster.

How do you respond to Alphonse's suggestion?

COMMENT

This chapter deepens Victor's inner conflicts. Although he feels a duty towards the monster he also feels guilty for endangering humanity.

Compare a similar mood in Chapter 9.

Recall his delays in Chapter 6.

Caught between these divided responsibilities, he deceives himself by delaying his work and avoiding his family. Notice how this conflict increases his isolation.

His isolation forms an ironic parallel to the monster's.

Victor's problems heighten and become more urgent when Alphonse proposes 'immediate marriage' to Elizabeth. His wish to please his aging father and his need to honour his mother's dying wish, conflict with his plans to create the female. This causes tension and suspense.

Alphonse's suspicion that Victor loves another woman is a powerful **dramatic irony** (see Literary Terms). We know that he is 'bound' by 'indissoluble ties' to the creature (p. 95).

Clerval is used to present Victor with an image of his 'former self'. Clerval's joy and 'enthusiastic imagination' only deepen Victor's gloom and serve to remind us of the contrast between the destinies of these two characters.

CHAPTER 19

The remoteness of this setting recalls the isolation of Walton.

In October, Victor and Clerval arrive in London and stay there until March. Victor, feeling guilty about the past and fearing the future, avoids company as much as possible. Eventually, they take a journey to Edinburgh and stop off at various places on the way. Victor leaves Clerval and goes to the remote Orkney islands; he is worried that he has delayed his task for so long that the monster might harm his family. He hires a shabby hut where he starts creating the new monster. This time, he is sickened and horrified by his work.

COMMENT

This chapter focuses on Victor's difficulty in dealing with the tension between his travels with Clerval and his need to create the female creature.

Victor is now depicted as the slave to the creature: 'I dared to shake off my chains' (p. 155).

Victor finds himself lured into 'peace' and 'happiness' by Clerval. He feels presumptuous because the creature has no friends and because he knows that making a second creature will cause him misery.

Victor deceives himself in a more surprising way. His claim that he was 'guiltless' (p. 157) is an astounding contradiction of all the facts.

Shelley develops an atmosphere of claustrophobia; Victor, who is 'embittered by the memory of the past

and the anticipation of the future' (p. 155) is clearly
haunted by the monster from all angles.

GLOSSARY   **Cumberland** the Lake District, home of the **Romantic** poets
                William Wordsworth and Samuel Taylor Coleridge
                amiable Falkland Lucius Cary (1610–43), a Royalist who fought
                for Charles I, and a humanist scholar
                insolent Goring George Goring (1608–57) kept switching sides
                between the Royalists and Puritans during the Civil War
                ennui world-weariness and depression of spirits
                Hampden John Hampden (1594–1643), leader of the
                opposition to Charles I
                superscription the name and address at the head of a letter

CHAPTER 20

One dark evening Victor has doubts. He thinks it
would be wrong to create another monster. When he
looks up, he sees the creature at the window, grinning,
and suddenly he destroys the half-finished monster.
The howling and anguished monster threatens Victor
but he remains firm in his decision not to create a
female companion. The creature leaves with the
haunting words, 'I will be with you on your wedding
night' (p. 163).

The storm   Victor sails out in a little boat and drops the remains of
symbolises the   the creature into the sea. He falls asleep in the boat.
monster's anger.   When he wakes, he finds that the high wind has taken
                     him far into the ocean. He eventually sees land and
                     arrives on the shore of Ireland. Strangers surround him
                     on the beach, accuse him of murder, and take him to
                     court.

COMMENT   This chapter signals a dramatic turning point in the
                 destinies of Victor and the monster.

Consider whether   The opening reveals Victor absorbed in his own
these doubts are   thoughts. His inability to escape from his own doubts
justified?   creates a mood of private claustrophobia.

The reader's sympathies are divided between Victor and the monster when the female is destroyed. We view this incident from both of their perspectives.

Do you feel grief or relief when Victor destroys the mate?

The window has a **symbolic** (see Literary Terms) role. It stands for the act of perception. it reveals as much about the perceiver as the thing perceived. The reader questions Victor's view that the monster is full of 'treachery' (p. 161).

Victor's destruction of the female is **symbolic**. Most female characters in the book are life-givers whereas the male characters appear ambitious and destructive.

Recall the ruthless attacks on the monster.

When Victor arrives in Ireland, parallels between Victor and the monster are strengthened. Victor, now a foreigner, is not welcomed by the prejudiced and suspicious crowd. He now feels what it is to be like an innocent victim.

GLOSSARY   **sophisms** eloquent but deceptive arguments

CHAPTER 21

Victor is in court. Witnesses come forward to give their evidence against him. He remains calm when the first man relates how he found a dead body on the beach until he mentions that there were black fingermarks on the neck. Realising that his monster has done the deed, Victor almost faints but this arouses the suspicion of the magistrate, who asks Victor to see the corpse, wanting to observe his reaction. It is the corpse of Clerval. Victor falls ill and spends two months in a prison cell. His fever is so strong he is barely conscious of his surroundings. He recovers and the magistrate tells him that evidence has been found which proves his innocence. Alphonse arrives and takes Victor on the journey back home.

The monster's revenge gathers apace.

COMMENT

Recall Justine's distraction when she is accused.

Forming a clear parallel to Chapter 8, Victor now replaces Justine as the victim on trial. When the magistrate reveals Clerval's body in order to judge Victor's reaction, Victor's shock arouses more suspicion. The moral themes of crime, justice, and freedom are developed as the prison takes on a **symbolic** role (see Themes). Victor's imprisonment mirrors the monster's lack of freedom in his hovel. The mental barrier that Victor felt between himself and society (p. 153) now becomes a shocking reality.

Victor is relieved from his despair by his father. Shelley contrasts this incident with the birth of the creature by repeating the **motif** (see Literary Terms) of the 'hand' 'stretched out'. Unlike Alphonse, Victor ran away from his son.

Victor's indulgence in laudanum stresses his **Romantic** (see Literary Terms) need for oblivion.

GLOSSARY

assizes court sessions
maladie du pays homesickness
laudanum a medicine which includes opium

CHAPTER 22

Victor has a rest from the journey in Paris. Alphonse is worried by Victor's habit of shutting himself away from company and blaming himself for the deaths of Justine and William.

In May, Victor receives a letter from Elizabeth. She declares her love for him but is anxious to know whether he is in love with another woman. The letter reminds him of the monster's threat, 'I will be with you on your wedding night', but he writes back expressing *Victor's secrecy* his love for her and his wish to be married. However, *upsets Elizabeth.* he warns her that he has a secret which he will tell her after the wedding.

When Victor and Alphonse arrive in Geneva, preparations are made, and Elizabeth is married to Victor. They decide to go to Italy by boat for their honeymoon. They enjoy the beautiful scenery and stop in Evian for the night. The sun is gradually sinking.

COMMENT

Victor's tragic blindness reaches new heights and fills the reader with a sense of oncoming catastrophe.

Victor's guilt is misplaced. He is disturbed by the fact that he created the monster when he should see that his failure to act as a parent to the monster has caused the deaths of William, Justine and Clerval.

Elizabeth's letter speeds up the marriage subplot and, in turn, the oncoming conflict promised by the monster.

Victor's misinterpretation of the monster's words, 'I will be with you on your wedding night' reveals Victor's deepening self-absorption. His belief that the monster will kill him, rather than Elizabeth, has a peculiar **dramatic irony** (see Literary Terms).

CHAPTER 23

How do you feel about the monster's revenge?

It is their wedding night. The moon appears and the wind rises. Terrified in the darkness and awaiting his own death, Victor spends an hour looking around the house for the monster. He is happy that it is nowhere to be seen. Suddenly he hears Elizabeth scream from the bedroom. He finds her dead with black fingermarks on her neck. He sees the monster grinning at the window and shoots at him. Victor assembles a party of people from the inn and they pursue the monster but fail to find him.

Victor returns to Geneva with the miserable news. The misfortune is too much for Alphonse, who dies.

Victor's last resort is to tell a magistrate the whole story of the creation and the monster's foul deeds, hoping that the law will hunt him down. The magistrate promises the monster will be suitably punished should he ever be found.

COMMENT

Recall the association of the monster with the moon.

Shelley creates tension in the reader by the dark **atmosphere** (see Literary Terms) of the storm and the blind nervousness of Victor.

The murder of Elizabeth is a dramatic scene. The fact that Victor is away from her and only hears the scream is thrilling.

The destruction of Elizabeth is a clear parallel to Victor's destruction of the monster's female companion. Now, however, the tables are turned.

The death of Alphonse strengthens the likeness between Victor and the monster: they both lack family and friends. They also become linked by their mutual revenge, when Victor decides to pursue the monster (see Themes).

The judge's disbelief of Victor's story blasts his final hope of justice.

CHAPTER 24

Note the irony of the Gothic setting (see Literary Terms).

Victor, furious for revenge, resolves to kill the monster or die in the attempt and is prepared to chase him across the world. Before he leaves Geneva, he goes to the graveyard and calls on the spirits of the dead to help him in his revenge. He hears the monster's laugh bellow in his ears.

Victor pursues the monster for months over land and sea. When Victor loses his tracks the monster taunts him by leaving signs and messages. This only serves to deepen Victor's passion to kill him.

Travelling towards the North Pole, Victor hires a sledge and dogs to chase his enemy. He almost catches him but they are separated when the ice splits apart. Victor find himself sinking when he sees Walton's ship.

Victor ends his narrative by pleading with Walton to kill the monster if he ever sees him.

COMMENT

The scope of the **setting** (see Literary Terms) becomes global as Victor and the monster chase each other.

There is a confusion of roles: it is difficult to decide which character has the upper hand and who is pursuing whom. Victor pursues the monster in a sledge but the monster taunts Victor in the graveyard and leaves him food to keep him alive.

Collect evidence showing Victor's determination and torment.

The monster's actions clearly suggest that he wants Victor to experience, and suffer, the same fate as himself. The two characters seem to merge: they are both isolated, hate each other, but are also fatally linked.

Notice that Shelley reveals how revenge is self-destructive: 'I was cursed by some devil and carried about me my eternal hell' (p. 197).

Victor's sighting of the ship brings us back to the start of the book from a new perspective.

Victor's request that Walton should destroy the creature is crucial to setting up the final climax of the novel.

A *Identify the speaker.*

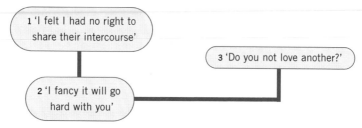

1 'I felt I had no right to share their intercourse'

2 'I fancy it will go hard with you'

3 'Do you not love another?'

Identify the person 'to whom' this comment refers.

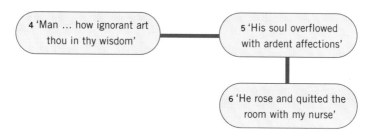

4 'Man ... how ignorant art thou in thy wisdom'

5 'His soul overflowed with ardent affections'

6 'He rose and quitted the room with my nurse'

Check your answers on page 96.

B *Consider these issues.*

a Similarities and differences between Victor's behaviour in Chapters 6–9 and 17–20.

b How the past affects the present.

c How the reader's sympathies are divided between Victor and the monster.

d How the idea of victimisation and prejudice have been portrayed. Which characters are victims of outside forces and how their experiences compare.

e The mood-pattern of the book: where are the climaxes and how Shelley has created the tension.

f The growing likeness between Victor and the monster.

g How the deterioration of Victor's family is presented.

Walton's second narrative (the final letters)

26 August
'Lost in the
darkness and
distance'

Walton resumes as the **narrator** (see Literary Terms).
He tells Margaret that Victor told this strange story
with great passion but admits that he would not have
believed it to be true unless Victor had shown him the
letters between Felix and Safie. He laments that Victor
must have been a great man before his misfortunes and
is worried that Victor's health is declining.

2 September

Walton's ship is surrounded by huge glaciers. Although
they are stuck, Victor rouses the hopes of the sailors.

5 September

Note similarities
between this speech
and Waldman's in
Chapter 3.

Still surrounded, Walton's crew threaten to mutiny
unless he decides to abandon his expedition once the
ice moves. Victor, however, gives a rousing speech,
urging them to continue their great enterprise. He tells
them it is shameful to abandon a glorious pursuit at the
first sight of danger. The crew appear moved by his
opinion.

7 September

Walton eventually gives way to the crew's wishes and
agrees to return to England if the ice clears.

12 September

The ice has cleared and Walton is returning to England
disappointed that his friend, Victor Frankenstein, has
died. Victor believed, in his last moments, that he was
not blameworthy for the monster's actions but urged
Walton to avoid ambition. While Walton is writing the
account of his death he hears a strange noise from
Victor's cabin.

Do you think his
speeches are a
satisfactory
conclusion to the
debates raised in
the book?

In Victor's cabin he meets the monster who seems both
gleeful at the death of Victor and upset. Walton accuses
him of hypocrisy. The monster replies that he cannot
believe how he has been a murderer because he started
his life with the intention of doing good and
experiencing life in the company of mankind. He
reminds Walton that mankind has only given him hate
for his good actions and that he has been a sufferer of

the worst injustices. He is so disgusted by his deeds of revenge that there is now only one course of action: he must kill himself. The monster then climbs out of the window and disappears into the darkness.

COMMENT   The narrative comes back full circle as Robert Walton provides us with the final and unexpected climax to the novel.

26 August   Walton portrays Victor as a tragic figure: a great man who has become a wreck and who knows the 'greatness of his fall' (p. 203).

Victor is a **Romantic** (see Literary Terms) hero. Despite his moral tale on the dangers of knowledge and ambition he still feels the need to be 'engaged in any high undertaking' (p. 205).

2 September   Walton appears to have learned from Victor's tale. Faced with the prospect of sinking, he realises that he has endangered the lives of his crew and his 'mad schemes are the cause' (p. 205).

5 September   Walton's reaction to his crew's threats mirrors Victor's initial response to the creature: Walton cannot 'in justice … refuse this demand'. It is **ironic** (see Literary Terms) that Victor seems ignorant of the moral of his

own tale when he makes his elevated speech, urging on
the crew.

7 September   The **ironies** deepen when Walton, who is responsible
for the fate of his crew, feels that he has been made a
victim of their unfair demands.

12 September   Victor's last words show his inability to accept his moral
message to 'avoid ambition' for he realises that 'another
may succeed' in 'science and discoveries' (p. 210).

Walton's despondency at losing his friend, and his
desire to carry out Victor's dying wish to destroy the
monster explain his reproaches to the creature.

The monster's final **Romantic** (see Literary Terms)
speech sums up the tragedy and the issues of the book.
It shows the contrast between his early goodness and
his evil revenge. It explains clearly that his rejection
by his creator and the rest of humanity was an 'injustice'
(p. 213).

The **Romantic** images and contrasts between joy and
despair, good and evil, light and darkness create a
powerful impact on the reader's imagination (see
Language).

The reader is finally left uncertain whether the monster
fulfils his promise to burn himself, for he is 'lost in
darkness and distance' (p. 215).

GLOSSARY   **Evil thenceforth became my good** recalls Satan's 'Evil be thou my
good' in *Paradise Lost*, Book 4.110

Identify the speaker.

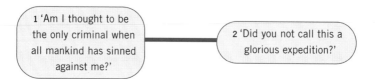

1 'Am I thought to be the only criminal when all mankind has sinned against me?'

2 'Did you not call this a glorious expedition?'

Identify the person 'to whom' this comment refers.

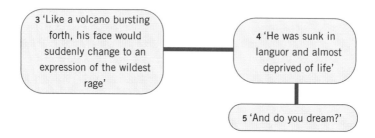

3 'Like a volcano bursting forth, his face would suddenly change to an expression of the wildest rage'

4 'He was sunk in languor and almost deprived of life'

5 'And do you dream?'

Check your answers on page 96.

 Consider these issues.

a The part played by references to heaven and hell in emphasising the duality and inner conflict of mankind.

b How examples of the **sublime** emphasise the uncertainty of the novel.

c How the structure of the novel is handled. How it is patterned and how it affects the reader.

d Whether the ending is a satisfactory conclusion to the book.

e How a fear of difference brings out the worst qualities in mankind.

f Whether the monster and Victor can be seen as tragic.

g The **symbolism** of Walton's voyage and the mutiny on board. How these relate to key themes.

h The ways that the three **narrators** can be seen as unreliable.

PART THREE

COMMENTARY

THEMES

THE MEANING OF THE MONSTER

At the heart of *Frankenstein* are a number of questions:
the monster asks 'Who was I?' and 'What was I?' The
answers still remain an enticing mystery. Many readers
have put forward different views.

Frankenstein can be read on many levels. The novel has
been seen as:

- A moral tale: a parable about the conflict between
  good and evil, or a warning about the dangers of
  scientific progress.
- A **Romantic** tale: the novel explores the tragic ruin of
  two heroes. Victor and the monster become powerful
  symbols (see Literary Terms) of loneliness who are
  destroyed by their own talents and needs.
- A psychological tale: the monster stands for the
  destructive quality of 'unnatural' desires and
  dangerous ambitions, or the dark side of Victor's
  personality on the rampage.
- A social tale: it is about a parent/child relationship
  showing the sad consequences of a father failing to
  perform his duties.

Remember the monster is made from the parts of many people.

- A political tale: the monster **symbolises** people who
  have been denied their natural rights of freedom,
  equality and fraternity. Victor stands for a tyrannical
  ruler (see Context & Setting).
- A philosophical tale: which asks 'What is the origin
  of evil?' Does it arise from our nature or does it come
  from the world around us – from society? The
  creature begins as a good character but becomes a
  monster by the cruel and monstrous ways humans
  treat him (see Context & Setting).

The best way for you to develop your own interpretation is to study the themes of the book and how they are developed by looking at:

• Events and how they are portrayed.
• Characters, their views, and how they are portrayed.
• Key images which are repeated in the language.

The main themes are: knowledge, ambition, prejudice, justice.

KNOWLEDGE

Discovery

Walton, Victor and the monster all begin their stories by expressing a deep desire to explain the world around them, which is like an unknown mystery waiting to be discovered (see Language). Each has a different focus. The monster wants to 'discover the motives' behind the De Laceys' behaviour and to 'unravel the mystery' of language. His humble aims are human, social, and arise from necessity. Victor and Walton, however, have lofty ambitions and are prepared to sacrifice human relationships in order to fulfil them. Victor's 'eager desire' to find the 'hidden laws of nature' and Walton's 'ardent' passion to explore the 'undiscovered solitudes' of the North Pole take them away from their loved ones and into isolation. However, their sacrifices are much deeper and more disturbing than this.

AMBITION

They become blinded by the strength of their own imaginations.

The central concern of the book are the moral consequences of ambition. Walton and Victor may have good intentions to be 'benefactors' to mankind by discovering great things, but as a result Victor destroys himself and those around him, and Walton puts his crew at risk. They fall victims to their uncontrollable passion to realise their dreams. Both characters are only

They both lack self-knowledge. partially aware of their surroundings and what they are doing. Victor is only able to see with hindsight that his experiments on corpses are immoral and 'unhallowed acts' and Walton's fantasy that 'snow and frost are banished' (p. 13) from the North Pole is shown in stark contrast to the real facts.

They act irresponsibly. Real problems occur when the ambitions of Victor and Walton endanger the lives of other people. Unlike Victor, Walton abandons his 'mad schemes'. He saves his crew, but reluctantly. Victor, however, is so 'wrapped up' in the process of making his creature, that he fails even to consider what his responsibilities towards it will be once it comes alive. Victor's ambitions are 'selfish' and quite the opposite of a benefit to mankind!

PREJUDICE

There are many examples in the book of characters who are prejudged, misunderstood and victimised by others, which leads to their rejection, isolation and despair.

Social corruption Justine, the Turkish Merchant and Victor are oppressed by people who crassly abuse their authority. Justine is wrongly put to death by judges who 'had rather ten innocent should suffer than one guilty should escape' (p. 82). She is also forced to confess a lie by a priest. Similarly, the Turk is condemned to death because the French authorities dislike his race, values and culture, which are different from their own.

Fear of difference People's fear of things which are unknown to them or which they do not understand, can bring out the worst in them – namely, mental cruelty and physical violence. People oppress other people by attacking, excluding, or imprisoning them, in order to control the source of this fear. Victor is treated roughly and brought in front of a magistrate by the suspicious Irish crowd because he is foreign. Justine is tormented by the crowd because they have already labelled her a child-murderer. Most obviously, the monster is beaten by the villagers because of his ugly physical appearance. They do not judge him by his actions or seek to understand him.

Imprisonment   The prison is an important **symbol** (see Literary Terms). The imprisonment of Justine and Victor are injustices because they are both innocent. The monster has to retreat into a hovel, a **symbol** of his social exclusion, rejection and isolation. It is his prison.

Viewpoint   People's inability to see the true reality beneath the appearance of things is a central theme. The window or frame is a **symbol** of how we view things. Many characters are mentally imprisoned by their own

Think how viewpoint affects the way things are described.   perspectives. Until Chapter 11, we see the monster as a 'devil' because this is how Victor sees him. We get a big shock when the monster speaks. His thoughts are beautiful. When Victor sees him at the window of his hut in the Orkneys he describes him as full of 'treachery'. We do not believe him. It is only now we see that Victor's prejudices have clouded his judgement. There are two perspectives of the creature: a 'feeling and kind friend' or a 'detestable monster' (p. 129). William, the nurse, Felix, the old man, the peasant, Mr Kirwin and the Turk all have limited viewpoints.

The monster in man   There are many instances when we feel that the humans are more monstrous than the monster. Shelley could be using the monster as a **symbol** for our own inner ugliness or the animal side of man's nature.

Other Gothic novels use this idea (see Broader Perspectives).   Although the monster appears to be the cause of fear and prejudice, he might stand for our ugly and violent reaction to something unknown and different.

JUSTICE

The source of conflict between Victor and the monster is explored thoroughly in their arguments in Chapters 10 and 17. The monster knows that he has been the victim of foul injustices at the hands of humans and he wants Victor to correct these wrongs.

Parental duties

The monster sees himself as the son of Victor when he says: 'I am thy creature: I ought to be thy Adam, but I am rather the fallen angel', and demands that Victor fulfil his 'duty' as a father. His deeds of revenge and mischief are due to pain, suffering and abandonment; this makes Victor partially responsible for the deaths of William and Justine. Victor cannot give the monster friendship because he cannot forgive him for William's murder. However, Victor does realise that he has 'no right' to withhold the gift of a female creature and that it would be 'justice' to create her (pp. 142–3). To deny him a mate is to deny him of his natural right to fraternity (see Context & Setting).

Companion-ship

Find scenes and incidents which show the effects of friendship.

The need for love, whether from friends, family or a partner, is a crucial issue in the novel. Victor's early years are portrayed as a paradise. Unlike the monster, he has no longing for love and affection because his parents 'overflowed with kindness'. Close relationships are depicted as a life-giving force. There are many instances of one character being 'restored to life' by the kind acts of another. Walton and Clerval both restore Victor to life and Safie restores the 'spirits' of Felix. Nature is also seen as a friend with the power to lift a human out of gloom and anxiety. Victor brings the creature back to life but fails to act as his friend.

Denial and guilt

Like Justine's mother, Victor is 'very vacillating' in his 'repentance'. He is caught in a vicious cycle between his duty to the monster and his duty to friends, family and mankind at large. He has no hard evidence of the

monster's good deeds, only evidence of bad ones. He
begins to distrust the monster and starts to have doubts
about his promise. He first thinks that he would be
saving mankind from the monster's revenge if he makes
the creature a mate, but changes his mind when he
considers that the monster might be just tricking him.
His destruction of the female mate is tragic and is a
consequence of Victor's growing paranoia and self-
absorption, which in turn is a consequence of his guilt.
Victor's feeling that he has 'unchained an enemy'
(p. 179) among his family and friends makes him
avoid them. Victor's inability to face up to his actions
and tell his secret to someone ruins his relationships
before the monster causes devastation.

Find evidence of his guilt in Chapters 9 and 18.

Revenge and destruction

Victor's refusal to make the female is a denial of the
creature's human rights. Victor does not treat him as a
human so he does not act like one. He truly lives up to
his name as a 'monster' and ceases to be a 'creature'.
The climax of the novel is taken up with the theme of
revenge. It is only by revenge and punishment that the
monster can feel that some justice has been done. He
evens up the score by subjecting Victor to the same
despair that he has experienced all his life. He kills his
friend. He sets Victor up as the suspect. Victor
experiences prejudice. Victor endures imprisonment.
Finally, the monster **symbolically** (see Literary Terms)
destroys Victor's female companion, Elizabeth. The
novel ends with them in mutual pursuit and combat.
These two characters become exactly like each other.
We do not know who is the monster and who is the
'victor'. We know from Shelley's diaries that she felt
revenge is a savage and destructive emotion and this is
made clear in the monster's final speech. He declares
tragically that he finds his crimes and his character
abhorrent. The only solution is suicide.

Find evidence of growing similarities between Victor and the monster.

STRUCTURE

The author shapes a novel to ensure that the purposes of the work are communicated effectively to the reader. He or she will choose to position events and ideas in a particular order and will decide to present them through particular forms.

Handling of time

The events in *Frankenstein* do not happen in chronological order. The novel begins after most of the action has already happened. To understand the mystery behind Walton's sighting of the creature and the decayed condition of Victor, the author returns to the past by using **flashbacks** (see Literary Terms). We go back to Victor's childhood and life at university but then William's murder creates a new mystery. In order to understand the lead-up to this event, Shelley turns the clock back to the early years of the monster. The two stories then converge. The final section of the novel explores the relationship between the creature and Victor. This brings us back full circle to the opening but we see Walton's ship from Victor's perspective this time. The very last section is the real dramatic climax to the novel where the three main male characters are brought together.

Find evidence to suggest the ending is predestined.

One effect of this technique is to show the influence the past has on the present. It emphasises how the fate of Victor and the monster are inseparable. This links to the theme of guilt: both the monster and Victor are haunted by their past actions, which keep returning in their minds and crush their spirits.

Narrators

Victor is the main narrator who tells Walton what the monster told him. Walton writes down for his sister what Victor told him. Each story is enfolded within another story: this is called **chinese-box narration** (see Literary Terms). This helps the reader feel that we are going deeper into the story; it shows that behind every

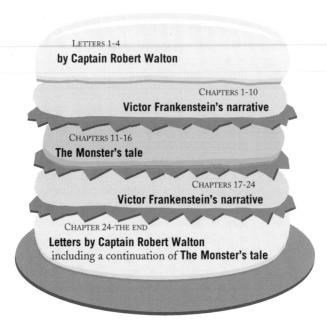

LETTERS 1-4
by Captain Robert Walton

CHAPTERS 1-10
Victor Frankenstein's narrative

CHAPTERS 11-16
The Monster's tale

CHAPTERS 17-24
Victor Frankenstein's narrative

CHAPTER 24-THE END
Letters by Captain Robert Walton
including a continuation of **The Monster's tale**

story there is another story told from a different point of view.

Shelley uses three narrators who tell their stories through their own eyes. We see the tale through different perspectives or angles. These viewpoints are all limited and biased, which helps us to make up our own minds about the characters and explore the novel with freedom. However, this technique does have a clear effect on our feelings: we feel sympathy for Victor in the first section, change our sympathies when we meet the monster, and experience divided sympathies in the final section.

Authenti-cation   The letters of Walton and his manuscript of the story make the extraordinary events appear more believable for us. Victor's evidence of the letters between Felix and

Safie, in turn, make Victor's story about the monsterseem more credible for Walton. Walton's meeting with the monster at the end of the tale finally vindicates Victor's tale. The story cannot be reduced to a delirious **fantasy** (see Literary Terms) of his deranged mind although Victor's wild style might have an edge of madness (see Language).

Contrasts and parallels Shelley structures her story by using contrasts and parallels. She loves repeating her ideas with slightly different variations. This forces the reader to relate the ideas together, and question the reason behind the links. These occur on many levels: language (see Language); characters (see Characters); **settings**; events and themes.

The most obvious contrast is between indoor and outdoor settings. Characters often occupy enclosed spaces: Victor's 'workshop' at the top of his house, his dilapidated hut in the Orkneys, the prisons, the monster's hovel, Walton's cabin, and the barn Justine sleeps in. These can stand as **symbols** (see Literary Terms) of mental as well as physical imprisonment. *Look at the description in Chapter 10.* Characters are also seen as travelling over vast expanses of land. Most scenes outside are barren, wild, or desolate: the North Pole, the Mer de Glace, the peaks of the Alps, the Orkney islands. These often **symbolise** the separation of a character from his fellow beings. Notice that Clerval's enthusiasm for nature is as much produced by his own imagination as it is by the nature of the scenes themselves.

Journeys form a pattern in the narrative. Often the story moves in cycles. Characters separate from others and return to meet them under different circumstances. Most obvious is the way the monster keeps returning to meet Victor. This creates a haunting feeling. Victor travels away from his family many times and always returns to them under new pressures.

Chapters often 'mirror' each other in the book. Here are some examples:

- 1 and 11 are concerned with the childhood of Victor and the monster.
- 2 and 12 focus on the curious minds of Victor and the monster.
- 8 and 21 Victor finds himself in the same position as Justine.
- 5 and 20 show the difference in Victor's attitude to creating the two creatures.
- 10 and 17 either side of the monster's story, Victor and the monster argue and discuss his needs.
- 6 and 18 show the difference in Victor's spirits as he journeys with Clerval.
- 9 and 18 reveal Victor's solitude, self-absorption and guilt.
- 18 and 23 two female companions are destroyed but the tables are turned.
- 12 and 16 show how the monster's bright hopes turn to dark despair and revenge.
- 2 and 24 show how Victor's bright hopes have turned to dark despair and revenge.

Shelley uses this device to show either how characters have been changed by events, or how characters have not changed but are faced with a different situation.

CHARACTERS

Think about these points as you study the following characters.

We can learn about characters by looking at:
- Their actions, behaviour, and the way they speak
- Their desires, values, and concerns
- How they view other characters, situations and events
- How other characters view them and talk to them
- Their relationships with other characters
- What the writer tells us or suggests to us

ROBERT WALTON

Walton is the narrator who begins the novel. Victor Frankenstein is first seen through his eyes.

There is little physical description of Walton. This makes us focus on his emotional qualities, mental characteristics and the way he tells his story – his **voice** (see Literary Terms).

Walton is an important character who serves many literary purposes:
- His concerns set up the main themes and issues
- He is used to prompt the main tale and close it
- His obvious similarities to Victor make us look for important differences

Compare his qualities to Victor Frankenstein's.

Walton, an ambitious man of twenty-eight, is portrayed as emotionally volatile and unpredictable. The passionate and joyful way he opens the novel, when he tells us how he imagines the North Pole, is offset by his claim that 'his spirits are often depressed'. Emotionally, too, his letters alternate between hope and gloom. Despite this, he is a determined character whose 'resolutions' are 'as fixed as fate'. At the end, his need to succeed on his voyage blinkers his understanding of his crew's threat of mutiny.

Walton is depicted as a **Romantic** (see Literary Terms) man. His strong imagination is a potential danger. His desire for exploration was first inspired by poems, books and childish fantasies. He is conscious that his 'daydreams' need to be controlled and yet appears incapable of controlling them himself (p. 18). This impractical sea-captain is prepared to sacrifice 'one man's life or death' in order to achieve his aims. His desires and ambitions prompt the main tale. The paths of Walton, Victor and the monster cross at the North Pole: it seems that this desolate **setting** is the only thing that can bring these unusual characters together.

Walton's need for a friend and his uncontrollable desire for new knowledge provide the perfect triggers for Victor's tale which explores how these two things are essentially at odds.

Shelley also uses similar imagery (see Language) and contrasts within language to link these two characters.

Shelley carefully shows how Walton and Victor are similar. They like each other immediately and Walton begins to 'love him as a brother'. Walton's prayers for a friend to regulate his mind seem to be answered with Victor, who is worried that Walton is 'pursuing the same course' as he did in the past: Victor does not want Walton's desire for knowledge to be a 'serpent to sting' him (p. 28). Walton, therefore, appears to be presented with an image of his potential future self: a man wrecked and destroyed by his own ambition.

Both characters fail to realise the effect their actions can have on others. Walton's feeling that the mutiny is an 'injustice' mirrors the relationship between Victor and the monster. The crew becomes the rebellious monster of Walton's creation that stands up for its own rights. It is **ironic** (see Literary Terms) that both characters feel themselves to be victims, yet both seem partially aware that their own 'mad schemes' are also to blame.

VICTOR FRANKENSTEIN

Victor is the second of the three narrators, and the central character of the novel.

Victor is loved by almost everyone: Caroline, Alphonse, Elizabeth, Ernest, Clerval, M. Krempe and M. Waldman, and even Mr Kirwin admire him. Walton introduces him as a 'celestial spirit', a 'divine wanderer', who has a 'never-failing power of judgment' (p. 28). Yet the reader knows these images only tell half the story. Either Mary Shelley was presenting us with a balanced view of Victor, or these **ironies** (see Literary Terms)

*Passionate and
introverted*

*Imaginative and
enthusiastic*

Single-minded

*Collect quotations
which illustrate
emotional tension
in Victor.*

*Find other scenes
and incidents
which show
Victor's lack of
self-awareness.*

simply reveal the short-sightedness of her other
characters.

The reader often feels **ambivalent** (see Literary Terms)
towards Victor. Like most tragic heroes, the traits of
personality which make him a powerful character are
the same traits which lead to his ruin.

We see early on that the combination of his 'thirst for
knowledge' and his 'child's blindness' will be dangerous.
We see the inner world of his mind blinding him to the
realities of the outer world in Chapter 4, when his
enthusiasm to discover the magnificent secrets of life
lead him to tamper with graveyards and dead bodies.
Furthermore, he is so buried in his work, he fails to
think of anything else: he forgets his family, abandons
daylight, and does not consider what he will do with
his creation once it is brought to life. Despite these
faults, the writing is so emotional and powerful, the
reader is taken away with Victor on his imaginative
journey and we also become 'exalted' (Chapters 3
and 4).

Victor seems either partially aware of his faults or
unable to admit to them. His own ambition and
passion for 'glory' are his worst enemies and he brings
devastation upon himself. His inability to recognise this
is seen by the way he blames outside influences such as
his university teachers and the books he has read for his
own downfall (Chapters 2 and 3). Although he
emphasises that his own future was predestined, he
hypocritically believes that Walton has the power to
change his future by controlling his passion for
knowledge.

Victor's self-contradictions become more frequent as his
problems become deeper. He alternately blames himself
and the monster for the deaths of William and Justine.
Divided between feelings of guilt and revenge, he

becomes at odds with himself. From Chapter 5, Victor
is portrayed as a gloomy and lonely spirit whose need
to keep the monster a secret creates an 'insurmountable
barrier' (p. 153) between himself and those he loves.
He has become the victim of his 'daemon'.

Consider your growing understanding of Victor's dilemmas. Think about the problems he faces over his relationship with the monster.

Our feelings towards Victor alter radically once we
meet the monster: Victor should feel more remorse for
abandoning the monster once he has created him.
Victor's duty towards his family and humanity would
have been better performed by doing his duty to the
monster (Chapters 17 and 20). A female companion
would remove the cause behind the monster's pain and
quell his desire for revenge. However, our sympathy for
the monster may lead us to underestimate the foulness
of William's murder. It is understandable that Victor
continues to see the monster as a 'devil' (Chapters 20
and 24).

Many of us may feel little pity for a character so
wrapped up in himself. To us, it seems obvious that the
monster's line 'I shall be with you on your wedding
night' is a threat to kill Elizabeth. Yet Shelley makes it
clear that Victor has not always thought of himself:
after Justine's death, he draws near to Elizabeth 'lest at
that very moment the destroyer had been near to rob
me of her' (p. 89). Victor's self-absorption grows as a
consequence of his genuine moral conflict (Chapters
18 and 19).

His death is truly tragic and **Romantic** (see Literary
Terms). Despite all Victor's warnings against ambition,
he still gives a rousing speech to the sailors, urging
them on to meet the dangers of the ice, and also dies
with the Romantic hope that another man might
succeed in knowledge where he had failed. Although
his desires have destroyed him, he cannot abandon his
true character in the face of death.

ALPHONSE

Alphonse Frankenstein, Victor's father, is depicted as a kind, gentle and respectable man of wealth. His loyalty to his friend Beaufort is shown by his determination to seek him out and his willingness to give him money and assistance. Alphonse also finds a secure home for the orphaned Caroline, whom he eventually marries.

The fathers of Clerval, Safie, Elizabeth, Caroline and the monster are all inadequate.

Furthermore, Victor sees him as a good father who fulfilled his responsibilities as a parent with an 'active spirit of tenderness' (p. 32).

However, Victor's account is one-sided. Later, it emerges that Alphonse is a distant and formal man: by the tone of his reproachful letters, and the way he sends Victor away to university in another country, despite his son's grief for Caroline (Chapters 3 and 4).

As a father he is not approachable. Victor cannot confide his real problems in him. Alphonse is motivated by his selfish desire to see Victor and Elizabeth married quickly.

ELIZABETH

Victor introduces Elizabeth as a 'beautiful and adored companion' (p. 34). Her desire to create strong relationships with others is seen by her friendships with Victor and Clerval (Chapter 2) and by the way she plays a mother to Victor's younger brothers (Chapter 6). Her goodness is shown by her effect on others, she 'softens' the ambitions of Clerval and is able to 'subdue' Victor's violent temper. Although she is gentle, she is also courageous. Her speech in court defending Justine is needed because other witnesses refuse to come forward out of fear of being associated with a child-murderer.

Elizabeth is a forward-thinking woman who has democratic values. She is proud of being Genevan and

Beautiful and good
Trusting and naïve

is happy to see equality between the classes in Switzerland (p. 63). However, she is also naïve and idealistic. Her belief in human goodness is shattered by Justine's unjust execution. She realises that 'vice' is not 'imaginary' but real (p. 88).

THE MONSTER

Hideous and at first well meaning
Vengeful when thwarted

The monster is a gigantic eight-foot-tall creature who has been made from the parts of dead bodies. When he is brought to life Victor achieves the impossible. The monster's unnatural creation, his ugliness and power are reflected in Victor's first descriptions of him as a 'daemoniacal corpse' and a 'daemon'. Victor portrays him as other-worldly later when he sees him in the Alps coming towards him at 'superhuman speed'. The monster's strength is seen in his physical endurance Chapter 24). Shelley's use of **satanic imagery** (see Literary Terms) to depict his emotions reveal him to be an evil character who should be feared. He appears to enjoy killing William and Elizabeth and is only satisfied when he reduces Victor to despair (Chapters 16, 23 and 24).

His merciless killing of Clerval, however, is the result of Victor's destruction of his half-finished female companion. The monster's fury and misery are the consequences of his loneliness and rejection by society. He begins life as an innocent and harmless being who has a natural attraction to humans. His child-like wonder and amazement at the world around him is beautiful and **Romantic** (Chapter 11 and 12). He loves nature, society and literature. He is a creature of good deeds: he collects wood for the De Laceys, saves a girl from drowning, and is a vegetarian!

His need for a friend is felt deeply. The brutal attacks on him by the villagers, Felix and the peasant who

Notice how Shelley uses the monster to discuss her concern for human rights.

shoots him, make us pity him. The barrier between himself and humanity is his physical ugliness, nothing more. This is seen when De Lacey accepts him for what he is, a lonely being who needs understanding. His demand for a companion is his last hope and a justice which Victor finally denies. The way he is mistreated by humans turns him from a creature into a monster.

We must not forget that the monster also has sexual feelings.

This imaginative and sensitive wanderer is essentially a **Romantic** (see Literary Terms) hero. His hope for a female is denied him because of his tragic error in killing William and his envious framing of Justine, acts which he later despises. His final speeches are elevated and noble. The vision he has of his own suicide is exalted and sublime (Chapter 24).

WILLIAM

Innocent and beautiful

Although William is a minor character, he has a huge impact on the book as a whole. He is the youngest son of Alphonse Frankenstein and is murdered by the monster because he refuses to be his friend. His death serves many literary purposes:

- It forces Victor to return home and encounter the monster on the way. His suspicion that the creature is the murderer raises expectations in the reader.
- It makes us sympathise with Victor. After overcoming the shock of the monster, this second misfortune follows quickly. His return to normal health is short-lived.
- It forms the basis of the subplot involving Justine. This allows Shelley to introduce political themes which are central to the relationship between Victor and the monster.
- The foulness of the murder makes Victor mistrust the monster. This mistrust makes him destroy the female creature.
- It shows how the monster is naïve in believing that William will be 'unprejudiced' (p. 137). Humans are

prejudiced from an early age and this is the root of
fear.
- It introduces the theme of mutual revenge between
Victor and the monster.

DE LACEY   At the heart of the novel is a kind and gentle old blind
man. He serves many literary purposes:
- His warm-hearted goodness to his family attract the
monster who pins all his future hopes of happiness on
befriending him.
- His poverty has not stopped him from loving his son,
Felix, who is responsible for it. He is the only
character who shows the capacity for forgiveness.
- The strong relationships he has created in his family
emphasise the monster's loneliness and make the
reader pity the creature.
- He is the only character in the book who shows the
monster any kindness. His blindness prevents him
from being prejudiced.
- The monster's desperation scares De Lacey and
makes Felix misinterpret the monster's intentions.

MINOR CHARACTERS

Minor characters enable the author to:
- Move the plot forward
- Develop a theme
- Help us to learn more about the major characters

The novel is populated with a great number of minor
characters who are used to mirror a quality of one, or
more, of the major characters. This prompts the reader
to question the difference between them. The minor
characters can be grouped together.

Virtuous   Caroline Beaufort's kindness towards the poor is a
women   'passion' rather than a 'duty' because she remembered
being the victim of poverty herself. Her adoption of the
Elizabeth recalls her own history. Like Caroline, the

orphans Elizabeth, Justine and Margaret all act as surrogate mothers. Agatha and Safie also show gentleness and kindness towards De Lacey and Felix. This kindness is precisely what the orphaned monster lacks.

Inadequate fathers

There are many fathers who, unlike the mothers, fail in their parental role. The fathers of Clerval, Walton, and Safie try to stop their children from pursuing their own interests. Their behaviour recalls Alphonse's dismissal of Victor's book. The Turk's tyrannical behaviour also mirrors Victor's attitude to the monster. Furthermore, the father of Elizabeth abandons her, and Caroline's father makes her suffer by his decision to hide from society after he lost his fortune. Their failures highlight Victor's more extreme failure to father the monster. All these fathers are different from De Lacey.

Ambitious sons

Felix, Clerval and Walton all have passionate ambitions to be 'benefactors' to mankind in some way. The plans of Felix cause suffering to his family and Walton's plans have the potential to be fatal. Clerval's seem harmless because of Elizabeth's influence. While women appear to be preserving and creating human relationships, men seem to destroy them. Again, these characters mirror Victor's dangerous but well-meaning ambitions.

Scientists

We see three scientists other than Victor. The first is Alphonse's friend, who explains electricity and galvanism. These become ideas central to Victor's work. M. Waldman also has a huge influence on Victor because he explains the miracles of modern science. The other lecturer, M. Krempe, recalls Alphonse by his sarcastic dismissal of Victor's passion for alchemy.

Judges

It is **symbolic** (see Literary Terms) that the only professional characters other than scientists are judges. This highlights the theme of how people judge each other and how the reader judges the characters.

Although they are responsible for the well-being of others, only Mr Kirwin decides to seek actively for the real truth. The judges in Chapters 8 and 23 are portrayed as short-sighted.

Crowds   There are three crowds of people: the people who hear the trial of Justine, the Irish crowd who accuse Victor of murder, and the villagers who attack the monster. All are brutal, short-sighted and dangerous.

LANGUAGE & STYLE

The author's choice of vocabulary and sentence-structure gives a novel a particular flavour. This has a direct, if subconscious, impact on the reader's imagination and feelings.

An important idea in the novel is the double-sided nature of mankind: man is both great and horrid. We all experience the tension between good and evil in our characters. These contrasts are reflected in Shelley's language.

'THE LANGUAGE OF MY HEART'

Walton, Victor and the monster all adopt an emotional style of writing to describe their experiences. Their passions are always extreme. Shelley uses four main devices to show this.

Descriptive   Shelley uses words which describe or are associated
language   with feelings, such as the monster's 'tears of sorrow and delight'. She often uses adjectives and adverbs to intensify their feelings: phrases like 'eagerly longed', 'frantic impulse', and 'ardently desired' roll off the page.

Metaphors   Shelley often compares her characters to other things.
and similes   Walton sees Victor as a 'gallant vessel' who is 'wrecked'. Victor, famously, compares his passion for science to a

'mountain river' which 'swelling as it proceeded …
became a torrent which in its course, has swept away all
my hopes and joys' (p. 37).

Contrasts

The three narrators have violent mood swings between
joy and despair. We can find these contrasts by:

- Comparing two passages: Victor's fascination for
  science in Chapter 4 contrasts sharply to his reaction
  to Justine's trial in Chapter 8. His 'imagination' is
  'exalted' and he is 'animated by an almost
  supernatural enthusiasm' for his work but he is filled
  with 'deep and bitter agony' and 'heart-sickening
  despair' when he realises its consequences.

Note contrasts in
Chapter 4.

- Looking for a contrast within a passage: when
  Walton talks with 'burning ardour' and becomes
  'warmed' with the 'fervour' of his voyage the mood
  suddenly changes as a 'dark gloom spreads' over
  Victor's face and a 'groan burst' from him (p. 27).

Collect examples of
this device for each
major character.

- Looking for contrasts within a sentence or a phrase:
  Victor often uses this device to emphasise his reversal
  in fortune – 'misfortune had tainted my mind and
  changed its bright visions of extensive usefulness into
  gloomy and narrow reflections upon self' (p. 37).

Rhetorical
language

Shelley uses repetition to build an emotional climax:
Victor's mind is 'filled with one thought, one
conception, one purpose'. She also uses different types
of sentences to create different moods. Walton's
question to Margaret shows amazement: 'do you not
feel your blood congeal with horror, like that which
even curdles like mine?' (p. 202). Victor's exclamations,
'Abhorred monster! Fiend that thou art!' here adds
emphasis to his insults.

KEY IMAGES

There are particular images which are repeated
throughout the novel. These **motifs** (see Literary

Terms) recall another event and relate it to the present instance.

Hands There are many times when characters cover their eyes with their hands when confronted with the monster. This image of refusing to see could suggest Victor's denial of his responsibilities, his blindness to the world around him, or his self-denial in accepting his own monstrosity.

We also see the image of the outstretched hand which is a **symbol** (see Literary Terms) of the longing for human contact. Victor's need for his father is reciprocated whereas the monster's is not.

Finally we see hands as the agents of evil forces. Victor fails to shrink from his work as he 'dabbled among the unhallowed damps of the grave' (p. 52) but does so when he creates the female. Similarly, the monster's fingermarks on the necks of his victims is the dark evidence of strangulation – deeds which he later regrets.

Birth and death Characters are 'restored to life' throughout, by the kind actions of other humans (see Themes). Shelley was aware of the contemporary scientific debates about a human life-force: many references are made to the human 'spirit' and 'animation'(see Context & Setting). These images contrast with the apparent death-in-life gloom of Victor who wanders 'like an evil spirit'.

The moon and storms The moon is strongly related to the presence of the monster. It appears when the monster is created and is also the first object in his world that gives him pleasure. It has a more eerie effect when it appears after the monster has promised revenge.

Storms occur frequently and create a sense of foreboding and chaos. They add to the tense **Gothic atmosphere** (see Literary Terms). These may be a symbol of the wild and chaotic emotions of the three main characters.

Books	Books populate the novel and have an important influence in determining the characters' destinies. This influence is bound up with the importance of the imagination (see Themes) – books affect us when we can see the images in our mind's eye. Uncle Tom's seafaring books and Coleridge are crucial for Walton, Agrippa for Victor, Milton for the monster, and ancient tales of chivalry for Clerval.
Windows	Windows or frame-like structures are symbols for a viewpoint onto reality (see Themes). They also symbolise a barrier between the characters either side of the window.
Heaven and hell	Images of light and dark, heaven and hell, warmth and cold, fire and ice, high and low, and joy and despair can be traced throughout. All these images recall *Paradise Lost*. Often, one of these pairs will tend to trigger off all the other pairs. The 'serpent' and the 'apple' which was 'already eaten' (p. 182) suggest that dark forces are at work, forces which will send the characters into despair.

IRONY

Collect a list of examples of ironic twists.

Shelley's use of irony and dramatic irony (see Literary Terms) abound in the novel. She uses it to help the reader take a critical attitude towards the narrators. Shelley does not interfere directly with the narrative but calmly points out contradictions, denials and hypocrisies in her characters by using twists in the tale.

PART FOUR

STUDY SKILLS

HOW TO USE QUOTATIONS

One of the secrets of success in writing essays is the way you use quotations. There are five basic principles:

- Put inverted commas at the beginning and end of the quotation
- Write the quotation exactly as it appears in the original
- Do not use a quotation that repeats what you have just written
- Use the quotation so that it fits into your sentence
- Keep the quotation as short as possible

Quotations should be used to develop the line of thought in your essays.

Your comment should not duplicate what is in your quotation. For example:

> Victor, in his struggle to decide whether to create the female mate for the creature, finally realises that he has no right to withhold happiness from him. He says, 'I had no right to withhold from him the small portion of happiness which was yet in my power to bestow.'

Far more effective is to write:

> Victor, in his struggle to decide whether to create the female mate for the creature, finally realises that he 'had no right to withhold from him the small portion of happiness' that was in his 'power to bestow'.

However, the most sophisticated way of using the writer's words is to embed them into your sentence:

> Victor, after having many doubts, finally realises that he has 'no right to withhold' the female mate from the creature and, in granting the creature's request, he would bestow the 'small portion of happiness' on him that is 'yet in his power'.

When you use quotations in this way, you are demonstrating the ability to use text as evidence to support your ideas - not simply including words from the original to prove you have read it.

Everyone writes differently. Work through the suggestions given here and adapt the advice to suit your own style and interests. This will improve your essay-writing skills and allow your personal voice to emerge.

The following points indicate in ascending order the skills of essay writing:

- Picking out one or two facts about the story and adding the odd detail
- Writing about the text by retelling the story
- Retelling the story and adding a quotation here and there
- Organising an answer which explains what is happening in the text and giving quotations to support what you write

....

- Writing in such a way as to show that you have thought about the intentions of the writer of the text and that you understand the techniques used
- Writing at some length, giving your viewpoint on the text and commenting by picking out details to support your views
- Looking at the text as a work of art, demonstrating clear critical judgement and explaining to the reader of your essay how the enjoyment of the text is assisted by literary devices, linguistic effects and psychological insights; showing how the text relates to the time when it was written

The dotted line above represents the division between lower- and higher-level grades. Higher-level performance begins when you start to consider your response as a reader of the text. The highest level is reached when you offer an enthusiastic personal response and show how this piece of literature is a product of its time.

Coursework essay

Set aside an hour or so at the start of your work to plan what you have to do.

- List all the points you feel are needed to cover the task. Collect page references of information and quotations that will support what you have to say. A helpful tool is the highlighter pen: this saves painstaking copying and enables you to target precisely what you want to use.
- Focus on what you consider to be the main points of the essay. Try to sum up your argument in a single sentence, which could be the closing sentence of your essay. Depending on the essay title, it could be a statement about a character: The traits of Victor's personality which make him a powerful character are also those which lead to his ruin; an opinion about setting: The frequent storms create a sense of foreboding and chaos; or a judgement on a theme: Walton, Victor and the monster all depict the world as an unknown mystery waiting to be discovered.
- Make a short essay plan. Use the first paragraph to introduce the argument you wish to make. In the following paragraphs develop this argument with details, examples and other possible points of view. Sum up your argument in the last paragraph. Check you have answered the question.
- Write the essay, remembering all the time the central point you are making.
- On completion, go back over what you have written to eliminate careless errors and improve expression. Read it aloud to yourself, or, if you are feeling more confident, to a relative or friend.

If you can, try to type your essay, using a word processor. This will allow you to correct and improve your writing without spoiling its appearance.

Examination
essay

The essay written in an examination often carries more marks than the coursework essay even though it is written under considerable time pressure.

In the revision period build up notes on various aspects of the text you are using. Fortunately, in acquiring this set of York Notes on *Frankenstein*, you have made a prudent beginning! York Notes are set out to give you vital information and help you to construct your personal overview of the text.

Make notes with appropriate quotations about the key issues of the set text. Go into the examination knowing your text and having a clear set of opinions about it.

In most English Literature examinations you can take in copies of your set books. This in an enormous advantage although it may lull you into a false sense of security. Beware! There is simply not enough time in an examination to read the book from scratch.

In the
examination

- Read the question paper carefully and remind yourself what you have to do.
- Look at the questions on your set texts to select the one that most interests you and mentally work out the points you wish to stress.
- Remind yourself of the time available and how you are going to use it.
- Briefly map out a short plan in note form that will keep your writing on track and illustrate the key argument you want to make.
- Then set about writing it.
- When you have finished, check through to eliminate errors.

To summarise,
these are the
keys to success:

- **Know the text**
- **Have a clear understanding of and opinions on the storyline, characters, setting, themes and writer's concerns**
- **Select the right material**
- **Plan and write a clear response, continually bearing the question in mind**

A typical essay question on *Frankenstein* is followed by a sample essay plan in note form. This does not present the only answer to the question, so do not be afraid to include your own ideas, or exclude some of the following. Remember that quotations are essential to prove and illustrate the points you make.

In what ways does Mary Shelley make you sympathise with the monster?

Introduction Analyse the key elements of the question. The 'ways' of the question involves looking at Shelley's literary techniques, and the impact of these in creating pity for the monster. The monster is a complex character: his violent and cruel actions shock us but these actions are counterbalanced with kind actions.

Part 1 The monster is portrayed as an evil force in Chapters 5 and 7. These fearful expectations are developed by making him the suspect for William's murder. Justine's death is a consequence of the murder. The way she suffers and the despair that Victor and his family are put through shows the monster's capability for destruction.

Part 2 Our initial view of the monster is radically challenged and our sympathy for Victor undermined. Note our surprise at his speeches in Chapter 10. The monster's attempt at evoking sympathy is balanced by Victor's scepticism. Is the monster just a persuasive speaker who is hiding evil intentions? Explain how the monster is portrayed as a harmless, child-like and vulnerable being in Chapters 11 and 12. Notice how the loneliness and abandonment of the monster makes us read back and re-evaluate Victor's behaviour in Chapter 5.

The author's use of the monster as a narrator influences our feelings about him: we see things from the monster's viewpoint and we become involved with his feelings. We pity him when he sees himself in the pool:

it is Victor who is responsible for his ugliness. Characters hate him for his ugliness and do not give him a chance to show what he is really like – a good and sensitive being who needs a friend.

Part 3   Look at how the structure is important. It is a turning point when Felix beats him, after he has become emotionally involved in the lives of the De Laceys. Explain that his growing sensitivity to the world around him and what he reads makes him self-conscious of his difference. He puts all his hopes on the De Laceys. Their departure thwarts his plans.

Part 4   Victor Frankenstein becomes the focus of our anger in Chapter 16. Notice Shelley's cleverness when William is murdered: we feel more sympathy for the monster because William is portrayed as yet another prejudiced human! Explain how the monster's actions can be partially 'excused' because of the way humans have treated him. Emphasise the logic and justice of the monster's demands.

Part 5   Explain how Shelley uses characters to develop themes. Show how the monster's concerns relate to other characters. Explore how Shelley is concerned with imprisonment, prejudice, justice, and the duty of parents. Contrast how the orphans Caroline, Elizabeth and Walton have been accepted. Contrast how Safie, despite her cultural differences is accepted by the De Laceys. Contrast Victor's childhood with the monster's. Contrast Victor's friends Clerval and Elizabeth with the monster's lack of friends. Show how the monster can be seen as an innocent, outcast victim.

Part 6   As the story is finally unfolded, the reader's sympathies become split between Victor and the monster. Victor's delays in creating the female cause tension. We have divided feelings when he destroys her; conflicting sympathies when the monster, out of revenge, plunges

Victor into desolation. We see that the monster wants to make him suffer the same things he has suffered, yet this will not solve anything. Show how these actions really do turn him into a devilish monster.

Conclusion   Show your final opinion of the question. We are shown the innocence of the monster's childhood and this undermines our initial impressions of him. Shelley's narrative technique, the contrasts between him and the other characters, and depiction of the monster as a noble being make us have more sympathy for him than Victor. Her use of irony reveals Victor's essential lack of awareness and his dying comments show how little he has learned. Compare this with the final encounter between the monster and Walton and show the impact this has upon our sympathy.

FURTHER QUESTIONS

Make a plan as shown and attempt these questions:

1 How much sympathy does the writer make you have for Victor Frankenstein?

2 Examine the differences between the male and female characters in the novel.

3 The relationship between Victor and the monster is important to the novel. Trace the development of this relationship as the novel progresses, analysing the main points in its development.

4 What do you find interesting about Shelley's use of locations and nature in the novel? How does this enhance our understanding of the whole novel?

5 Explain how each of the major characters in the novel, Walton, Victor and the monster, is important to our understanding of what the novel is about.

6 In what ways is *Frankenstein* a book of the emotions and the imagination?

7 To what extent is Victor Frankenstein responsible for his own downfall? How does this link with the decline of the monster?

8 If you were Victor Frankenstein, would you create the female creature for the monster? Discuss the reasons behind your decision in detail.

9 How reliable, in your opinion, is Victor Frankenstein as a storyteller? You should consider his attitude and behaviour towards the monster, the effect of the monster's story on the reader, and Walton's confrontation with the monster.

10 Discuss Shelley's portrayal of the nature of good and evil and of the conflict of these forces in man's personality.

11 The monster has a powerful effect on all those who meet him. Compare De Lacey's reaction to the monster with the reactions of another two characters in the novel, explaining any differences and similarities that you see.

12 How does the way the story is told, with three narrators, affect the way the reader sees the novel?

PART FIVE

CULTURAL CONNECTIONS

BROADER PERSPECTIVES

*Other works
by the Shelleys*

*This novel
provided another
catastrophic theme
for later science-
fiction writers to
explore.*

The Mary Shelley Reader (Oxford University Press) contains a wide selection of her writings including short stories, her novella *Mathilda* about the incestuous relationship between a father and his daughter, and some essays and journals. Her other great novel is *The Last Man*, a futuristic fantasy concerned with the final destruction of the human race.

Percy Shelley's poems are emotionally powerful, imaginative, and at times, cosmic. Try 'Alastor', 'Mont Blanc', and 'Ozymandias', 'To a Skylark', and 'Ode to the West Wind'.

*Other
Romantics*

To help you understand the spirit of **Romanticism** (see Literary Terms), listen to the thunderstorm in Beethoven's 6th symphony after reading a storm scene in *Frankenstein*. Look at some paintings by the German painter, Caspar David Friedrich. Look at Henry Fuseli's painting 'The Nightmare' alongside the description of Elizabeth's death, and find similarities between Friedrich's 'The Wanderer over the Sea of Clouds' with Victor Frankenstein in Chapter 10. Read Wordsworth's 'I Wandered Lonely as a Cloud' to see how nature restores the spirit of man. See how Coleridge's 'Kubla Khan' compares with the idea that great visions are finally destroyed.

Compare the themes of revenge and imprisonment in Emily Brontë's novel *Wuthering Heights* to *Frankenstein*.

Gothic horror

For those of you addicted to terror, there are plenty of stories that will ensure a sleepless night. All the following books are also available on audio-cassette.
- The classic tale of a split personality is *Dr Jekyll and Mr Hyde* (Robert Louis Stevenson). Disastrous

Think whether these are just tales of terror or whether they reveal a deep and symbolic understanding of our fears and desires?

results ensue when the scientist, Dr Jekyll, discovers a potion that can awaken the hidden evil in man's nature. The pursuit for the violent criminal who haunts the streets of Victorian London is gradually unfolded by three different narrators in the form of legal documents.

• Edgar Allan Poe's mentally deranged narrators are known for their eccentricity, unreliability and intense states of mind. His claustrophobic *Tales of Mystery and Imagination* have been extremely influential in the way they play games with the reader. Everything from madness, hypnosis, premature burial to the misuse of dental surgery is featured in Poe's bizarre and horrific universe. Try his story 'The Black Cat' as a starting point.

• The attractive but cruel hero of *The Picture of Dorian Gray* (Oscar Wilde) makes a wish for eternal youth. Strangely, his wish comes true, but while his body remains young he is shocked to find that his portrait gradually changes into a sinister and wicked old man. This tale of murder, betrayal, opium-addiction, bribery and suicide is poetic, subtle and carefully crafted by its author.

• *Dracula* (Bram Stoker) is a nobleman doomed to eternal life who buys a property in England and begins a mysterious blood-sucking carnage. Told by many narrators in the form of journals, diaries and letters.

Biographies   Muriel Spark's *Mary Shelley* (Constable, 1993) remains the definitive biography, while the more intellectual *The Godwins and The Shelleys* by William St Clair (Faber, 1989) focuses on the whole family.

Criticism   Try reading:
Maurice Hindle's *Frankenstein: A Penguin Critical Study* (Penguin), certainly the most thorough textual analysis.

The York Note on *Dr Jekyll and Mr Hyde* by Tony Burke has an accessible section on the development of the Victorian horror story.

Film and video

The first in the BBC series *Nightmare: The Birth of Horror* by Christopher Frayling focuses on the writing of *Frankenstein* and how it has continued to haunt us; the accompanying book is well-illustrated and inspiring. The 1931 film version starring Boris Karloff is famed for its depiction of the creature as an uneducated zombie. The recent version starring Kenneth Branagh and Robert de Niro is more faithful apart from the spurious insertion of some love-scenes.

The Internet

Check out the following sites:
http://www.english.udel.edu/swilson/mws/mws.html
romantic web site, chronology and links
http://www.engl.virginia.edu/~enec981/Group/
chris.intro.html on the Gothic
http://www.desert-fairy.com/maryshel.html
definitely the best – comprehensive on life, sources, influences

Societies

If you are a horror fanatic then join The Gothic Society at Chatham House, Gosshill Road, Chislehurst, Kent. BR7 5NS. They have recently reprinted *Tales of the Dead*, the stories which inspired the ghost story competition at Byron's villa.

ambivalence when an author or character feels two opposite extremes of emotion at the same time

atmosphere a setting or situation's mood

Byronic the qualities pertaining to the rebellious heroes created by the poet, Lord Byron. They are usually gloomy, proud, and disdainful but also mysterious, attractive and magnetic

chinese-box narration when an author wraps a story inside of a story inside of another story you could liken this to a chinese box

Enlightenment in eighteenth-century France, a time when philosophers were convinced that the application of Reason would solve the problems of humanity. Reason was thought to lead naturally to scientific discovery. Mary Shelley's father, William Godwin, was a disciple of this intellectual movement

epic a long narrative poem, written in elevated style about the exploits of superhuman heroes

fantasy a kind of imagining, divorced from any contact with the real world of things and ideas

feminism a political movement which fights for women's equality and freedom from social and economic dependency upon men

flashback when the narration jumps backward in time to an earlier point in the story

genre a type or class of literature which follows the same form, e.g., horror, science-fiction, realism, spy-thriller

Gothic novel an influential literary genre that contains supernatural, unexplained and weird events in order to provoke either terror or horror in the reader. Its imagery is usually inspired by dreams and nightmares. It flourished 1765–1900, and, at the time, was far more popular than realism

imagery any language which requires the reader to form a mental picture

implied meaning the meaning beneath the surface

irony a 'tongue in cheek' piece of language where the meaning beneath the surface is in contrast with the apparent meaning. It is usually used so the author can make a subtle criticism of a character without intruding directly and obtrusively into the text. The effect can be either humorous, serious, or both

metaphor when two things are compared implicitly, e.g., Frankenstein is a 'gallant vessel' to Cpt Walton

motif an image, idea, or situation which recurs throughout the text forming a pattern, e.g., the association between the monster and the moon

multiple narration when a story is told using more than one narrator

multiple viewpoint when a story is told from the perspective of more than one character

narrator the story-teller

paradox when language or a state of affairs seems to contradict itself on the surface but makes sense underneath, e.g., it is paradoxical that the monster hates Frankenstein but cannot do without him

realism writing which deals in a down-to-earth way with ordinary life

rhetorical question a question that is asked in order to emphasise a point rather than expect an answer

Romantic an influential cultural movement in literature, music and painting (in the late eighteenth and early nineteenth centuries) that focused on the expression of sublime emotions aroused by nature, the imagination, dreams and solitude. Romantics include Byron, Turner, Blake, Wordsworth, Coleridge, the Shelleys and Keats, in Britain, and Beethoven, Schiller, Hoffmann and Goethe in Germany

satanic school the Romantic poets William Blake, Percy Shelley and Lord Byron thought that the character of Satan in *Paradise Lost* by John Milton should be seen as an attractive and justified rebel who was fighting against a tyrannical God for his own freedom

science-fiction an influential literary genre which concentrates on the way technological progress can and does affect mankind. Stories are often set in the future and have disastrous outcomes

setting the place or environment where the events in a story are set. Settings are sometimes used to create a mood, reflect a character's inner feelings, or used symbolically

simile when two things are compared by using the word 'like' or 'as'

sublime refers to a stimulus which arouses exalted emotions; it may be a feeling of overpowering joy or, alternatively, terror

symbolism when one image is used to mean something else, often an idea or emotion

uncanny an eerie feeling created by something seemingly supernatural

TEST ANSWERS

TEST YOURSELF (Letters 1–4)

A 1 Walton *(p. 16)*
2 Victor *(p. 27)*
3 Walton *(p. 14)*
4 The monster *(p. 23)*
5 Victor *(p. 24)*
6 Walton *(p. 25)*
7 Margaret *(p. 18)*

TEST YOURSELF (Chapters 1–5)

A 1 Alphonse *(p. 37)*
2 Waldman *(p. 46)*
3 Victor *(p. 53)*
4 Victor *(p. 54)*
5 Elizabeth *(p. 36)*
6 Clerval *(p. 36)*
7 The monster *(p. 56)*

TEST YOURSELF (Chapters 6–10)

A 1 Victor *(p. 86)*
2 Elizabeth *(p. 88)*
3 The monster *(p. 96)*
4 Elizabeth *(p. 75)*

5 Justine *(p. 79)*
6 Justine's mother *(p. 64)*

TEST YOURSELF (Chapters 11–16)

A 1 The monster *(p. 142)*
2 De Lacey *(p. 129)*
3 Justine *(p. 138)*
4 Safie *(p. 122)*
5 William *(p. 137)*
6 Felix *(p. 104)*

TEST YOURSELF (Chapters 17–24)

A 1 Victor *(p. 179)*
2 The nurse *(p. 172)*
3 Elizabeth *(p. 181)*
4 The judge *(p. 194)*
5 Clerval *(p. 151)*
6 Mr Kirwin *(p. 174)*

TEST YOURSELF (The Final Letters)

A 1 The monster *(p. 213)*
2 Victor *(p. 207)*
3 Victor *(p. 202)*
4 Victor *(p. 208)*
5 Walton *(p. 211)*